FUNDAMENTALS OF
ENGLISH
GRAMMAR
Second Edition

WORKBOOK Volume B

Betty Schrampfer Azar
Donald A. Azar

Longman

To Immee, Amelia Azar

Publisher: *Tina B. Carver*
Managing editor, production: *Sylvia Moore*
Editorial/production supervisor: *Janet Johnston*
Editiorial assistant: *Shelley Hartle*
Buyer and Scheduler: *Ray Keating*
Illustrator: *Don Martinetti*
Cover supervisor: *Marianne Frasco*
Cover designer: *Joel Mitnick Design*
Interior designer: *Ros Herion Freese*

Printed in the United States of America

10   9   8

ISBN 0-13-347089-X

Contents

Chapter 11 THE PASSIVE

Chapter 12   ADJECTIVE CLAUSES

Chapter 13   COMPARISONS

Chapter 14   NOUN CLAUSES

Chapter 15 QUOTED SPEECH AND REPORTED SPEECH

Chapter 16 USING WISH; USING *IF*

Preface

This *Workbook* consists of exercises to accompany *Fundamentals of English Grammar (2nd edition)*, a developmental skills text for mid-level ESL/EFL students. The exercises are designated SELFSTUDY (answers given) or GUIDED STUDY (answers not given). The SELFSTUDY practices are intended for students to use independently. The answers are in a separate, detachable *Answer Key* booklet at the back of this book. The GUIDED STUDY practices may be selected by the teacher for additional classwork, homework, or individualized instruction. Answers to the GUIDED STUDY practices, as well as suggestions for using the *Workbook,* can be found in the *Teacher's Guide.*

Many of the initial practices in each unit are tightly controlled and deliberate, intended to clarify form and meaning. Control is then loosened as the manipulative and clarifying practices lead to others that promote free, creative use of the target structures. The *Workbook* also contains suggestions for writing and various group activities such as games and discussions.

ACKNOWLEDGMENTS

I am grateful to the many people who enable me to pursue the work I love. I am especially indebted to my husband, mainstay, and co-author, Don, who kept me afloat through the recent illness and loss of my much loved mother and provided the support system in which our work together could continue and prosper.

I am also greatly indebted to Shelley Hartle, our editorial assistant, without whom it would have been impossible to keep to production schedule. Though still new to the team, she adapted quickly and handled everything with aplomb, from proofing galleys and compiling indexes to tending the ducks when we had to be away.

Many thanks to Janet Johnston, our production editor, who kept everything running smoothly on her end and was wonderfully supportive and understanding. Thanks similarly go to Sylvia Moore, managing editor. Special thanks also go to Tina Carver, publisher, who has been consistently supportive not only as a friend but as a top-notch publishing professional whose sound judgment I highly respect.

My appreciation goes, too, to Ray Adame, Barbara Barysh, Nancy Baxer, Eric Bredenberg, Karen Chiang, Athena Foley, Norman Harris, Terry Jennings, Gordon Johnson, Ray Keating, Andy Martin, Don Martinetti, Gil Muller, Ed Perez, Jack Ross, Jerry Smith, and Ed Stanford. In addition, my gratitude goes to Joy Edwards, Barbara Matthies, and R. T. Steltz. Chelsea Azar has been splendid. Finally, I am lovingly grateful to my father for his continuing support and involvement in my endeavors. Many of his ideas and suggestions are reflected in the text.

BETTY SCHRAMPFER AZAR

Once again, I begin by expressing my gratitude to Betty for her continued patience and guidance, and for the same incredible expertise that she brings to all phases of this project. Much of this was accomplished during a difficult time. Her ability and persistence got the book out. I continue to marvel and to learn.

I want to thank my father-in-law, Bill Schrampfer, for numerous handwritten ideas for topics and sentences. His agile mind provided much fodder. Inspiration appeared from many sources, R.T. Steltz, Tom Hemba, and my uncle Elias George among them, as well as Fred Lockyear, Gary Althen and other colleagues whose brains I often pick without knowing why until I start putting sentences down.

And special thanks still go to Chelsea Azar. She continues to endure our commitment to these projects and always provides joy and support.

DONALD A. AZAR

CHAPTER 9
Connecting Ideas

◇ PRACTICE 1—SELFSTUDY: Connecting ideas with *and.* (Chart 9-1)

Directions: <u>Underline</u> the words that are connected with **AND**. Label these words as NOUNS, VERBS, or ADJECTIVES.

     noun + noun + *noun*
1. The farmer has a <u>cow</u>, a <u>goat</u>, and a black <u>horse</u>.
    adjective + adjective
2. Danny is a <u>bright</u> and <u>happy</u> child.
 verb   *+ verb*
3. I <u>picked</u> up the telephone and <u>dialed</u> Steve's number.

4. The cook washed the vegetables and put them in boiling water.

5. My feet were cold and wet.

6. Sara is responsible, considerate, and trustworthy.

7. The three largest land animals are the elephant, the rhinoceros, and the hippopotamus.

8. A hippopotamus rests in water during the day and feeds on land at night.

◇ PRACTICE 2—SELFSTUDY: Punctuating a series with *and.* (Chart 9-1)

Directions: Add COMMAS where necessary.

1. Rivers streams lakes and oceans are all bodies of water.
   → *Rivers, streams, lakes, and oceans are all bodies of water.* OR
   Rivers, streams, lakes and oceans are all bodies of water.

2. My oldest brother my neighbor and I went shopping yesterday.

3. Ms. Parker is intelligent friendly and kind.

4. Did you bring copies of the annual report for Sue Dan Joe and Mary?

5. In the early 1600s, the Chinese made wallpaper by painting birds flowers and landscapes on large sheets of rice paper.

6. Can you watch television listen to the radio and read the newspaper at the same time?

7. Lawyers doctors teachers and accountants all have some form of continuing education throughout their careers.

8. Gold is beautiful workable indestructible and rare.

9. My mother father grandfather and sisters welcomed my brother and me home.

10. My husband imitates animal sounds for our children. He moos like a cow roars like a lion and barks like a dog.

◇ PRACTICE 3—GUIDED STUDY: Punctuating a series with *and.* (Chart 9-1)

Directions: Make a list for each of the topics below. Then write sentences using this list. Use AND in your sentence.

Example: three things you are afraid of
   List: heights
   poisonous snakes
   guns

Possible sentences:
   → *I'm afraid of heights, poisonous snakes, and guns.*
   → *Three of the things I'm afraid of are heights, poisonous snakes, and guns.*
   → *Heights, poisonous snakes, and guns make me feel afraid.*

1. your three favorite sports

2. three adjectives that describe a person whom you admire

3. four cities that you would like to visit

4. three characteristics that describe (*name of this city*)

5. three or more separate things you did this morning

6. the five most important people in your life

7. three or more things that make you happy

8. three or more adjectives that describe the people in your country

◇ PRACTICE 4—SELFSTUDY: Connecting ideas with *and*. (Chart 9-1)

Directions: Each of the following sentences contains two independent clauses. Find the SUBJECT (**S**) and VERB (**V**) of each clause. Add a COMMA or a PERIOD. CAPITALIZE as necessary.

     S **V**   **S** **V**
1. Birds fly**,** and fish swim.

     S **V**   **S** **V**
2. Birds fly**.** **F**/fish swim.

3. Dogs bark lions roar.

4. Dogs bark and lions roar.

5. A week has seven days a year has 365 days.

6. A week has seven days and a year has 365 days.

7. Bill raised his hand and the teacher pointed at him.

8. Bill raised his hand the teacher pointed at him.

◇ PRACTICE 5—SELFSTUDY: Using *and, but,* and *or*. (Chart 9-2)

Directions: Add COMMAS where appropriate.

1. I talked to Amy for a long time but she didn't listen.

 → *I talked to Amy for a long time***,** *but she didn't listen.*

2. I talked to Tom for a long time and asked him many questions.

 → *(no change)*

3. I talked to Bob for a long time and he listened carefully to every word.

 → *I talked to Bob for a long time***,** *and he listened carefully to every word.*

4. Please call Jane or Ted.

5. Please call Jane and Ted.

6. Please call Jane Ted or Anna.

7. Please call Jane Ted and Anna.

8. I waved at my friend but she didn't see me.

9. I waved at my friend and she waved back.

10. I waved at my friend and smiled at her.

11. Was the test hard or easy?

12. My test was short and easy but Ali's test was hard.

◇ PRACTICE 6—SELFSTUDY: Using *and, but, or,* and *so.* (Charts 9-1 → 9-3)

Directions: Write in the correct completion.

1. I was tired, _____**so**_____ I went to bed.
   A. but   B. or   C. so

2. I sat down on the sofa _____ opened the newspaper.
   A. but   B. and   C. so

3. The students were on time, _____ the teacher was late.
   A. but   B. or   C. so

4. I would like one pet. I'd like to have a dog _____ a cat.
   A. but   B. and   C. or

5. Our children are happy _____ healthy.
   A. but   B. and   C. or

6. I wanted a cup of tea, _____ I heated some water.
   A. but   B. and   C. so

7. The phone rang, _____ I didn't answer it.
   A. but   B. and   C. so

8. You can have an apple _____ an orange. Choose one.
   A. but   B. and   C. or

◇ PRACTICE 7—SELFSTUDY: Using *and, but, or,* and *so.* (Charts 9-1 → 9-3)

Directions: Add COMMAS where appropriate. Some sentences need no commas.

1. I washed and dried the dishes. → (*no change*)

2. I washed the dishes and my son dried them.

   → *I washed the dishes, and my son dried them.*

3. I called their house but no one answered the phone.

4. He offered me an apple or a peach.

5. I bought some apples peaches and bananas.

6. I was hungry so I ate an apple.

7. Bill was hungry and ate two apples.

8. My sister is generous and kind-hearted.

9. My daughter is affectionate shy independent and smart.

10. It started to rain so we went inside and watched television.

◇ PRACTICE 8—SELFSTUDY: Using *and, but, or,* and *so.* (Charts 9-1 → 9-3)

Directions: Add COMMAS where appropriate. Some sentences need no commas.

1. Gina wants a job as an air traffic controller. Every air traffic controller worldwide uses English so it is important for Gina to be fluent in the language.

2. Why do people with different cultural backgrounds sometimes fear and distrust each other?

3. Mozart was a great composer but he had a short and difficult life. During the last part of his life, he was penniless sick and unable to find work but he wrote music of lasting beauty and joy.

4. Nothing in nature stays the same forever. Today's land sea climate plants and animals are all part of a relentless process of change continuing through millions of years.

5. People and animals must share the earth and its resources.

6. According to one researcher, the twenty-five most common words in English are: *the and a to of I in was that it he you for had is with she has on at have but me my* and *not.*

◇ PRACTICE 9—SELFSTUDY: Separating sentences: periods and capital letters.
(Charts 9-1 → 9-3)

Directions: Add PERIODS and CAPITAL LETTERS as necessary.

1. There are over 100,000 kinds of flies they live thoughout the world.
   → *There are over 100,000 kinds of flies.* **T***hey live throughout the world.*

2. I like to get mail from my friends and family it is important to me.

3. We are all connected by our humanity we need to help each other we can all live in peace.

4. There was a bad flood in Hong Kong the streets became raging streams luckily no one died in the flood.

5. People have used needles since prehistoric times the first buttons appeared more than two thousand years ago zippers are a relatively recent invention the zipper was invented in 1890.

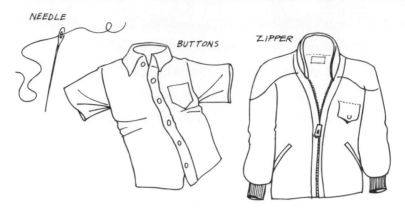

◇ PRACTICE 10—GUIDED STUDY: Punctuating with commas and periods. (Charts 9-1 → 9-3)

Directions: Add COMMAS, PERIODS, and CAPITAL LETTERS as necessary.

1. African elephants are larger than Asiatic elephants. Elephants native to Asia are easier to train and have gentler natures than African elephants.

2. Asiatic elephants live in jungles and forests in India Indonesia Malaysia Thailand India China and other countries in southeastern and southern Asia.

3. Elephants eat roots leaves bushes grass branches and fruit they especially like berries dates corn and sugar cane.

4. Elephants spend a lot of time in water and are good swimmers they take baths in rivers and lakes and like to roll around in muddy water they like to give themselves a shower by shooting water from their trunks.

5. After a bath, they often cover themselves with dirt the dirt protects their skin from the sun and insects.

6. Most elephants live in herds an older female (called a *matriarch*) leads a herd.

7. A female elephant is pregnant for approximately twenty months and almost always has only one baby a young elephant stays close to its mother for the first ten years of its life.

8. Elephants live peacefully together in herds but some elephants (called *rogues*) leave the herd and become mean these elephants usually are in pain from decayed teeth a disease or a wound.

9. Elephants are intelligent animals a well-trained elephant can kneel stand up or turn around on command.

10. Elephants are in danger of extinction so it is important to stop the illegal killing of elephants they are killed most often for their ivory.

◇ PRACTICE 11—GUIDED STUDY: Punctuating with commas and periods.
(Charts 9-1 → 9-3)

Directions: Add COMMAS, PERIODS, and CAPITAL LETTERS as necessary.

(1)   A a few days ago, a friend and I were driving from Benton Harbor to Chicago. W we were

(2)   in a lot of traffic, but it was moving smoothly. W we didn't experience any delays for the

(3)   first hour but near Chicago we ran into some highway construction the traffic wasn't moving at

(4)   all my friend and I sat in the car and waited we talked about our jobs our families and the

(5)   terrible traffic slowly the traffic started to move

(6)   we noticed a black sports car at the side of the road the right blinker was blinking the driver

(7)   obviously wanted to get back into the line of traffic car after car passed without letting the

(8)   black sports car get in line I decided to do a good deed so I motioned for the black car to get

(9)   in line ahead of me the driver of the black car waved thanks to me and I waved back at him all

(10)   cars had to stop at a toll booth a short way down the road I held out my money to pay my toll

(11)   but the tolltaker just smiled and waved me on she told me that the man in the black sports car

(12)   had already paid my toll wasn't that a nice way of saying thank you?

◇ PRACTICE 12—SELFSTUDY: Using auxiliary verbs after *but* and *and*. (Chart 9-4)

Directions: Complete the sentences with AUXILIARY VERBS.

PART I: Auxiliaries after *but*.

1. Debra **reads** a lot of books, but her brothers _____*don't*_____.

2. Sam **isn't** in the school play this year, but Adam _____*is*_____.

3. I **will be** at home this evening, but my roommate _____.

4. Ducks **like** to swim, but chickens _____.

5. That phone **doesn't work,** but this one _____.

6. Joe **is** at home, but his parents _____.

7. I **can't swim,** but my dog _____.

8. Jack **has visited** my home, but Linda _____.

9. I'm **not going** to graduate this year, but my best friend _____.

10. My dog **crawls** under the bed when it thunders, but my cat _____.

PART II: Auxiliaries after *and*.

11. Debra **reads** a lot of books, and her sisters _____*do*_____ too.

12. Horses **are** domesticated animals, and camels _____ too.

13. Red **isn't** a dull color, and orange _____ either.

14. Jack **didn't go** to the picnic, and Paul _____ either.

15. I **work** at an airplane factory, and my brother _____ too.

16. Dick **won't work** late every evening, and Jean _____ either.

17. Fatima **is** in class today, and Pedro _____ too.

18. I **can't** sing, and my wife _____ either.

◇ PRACTICE 13—SELFSTUDY: Using auxiliary verbs after *but* and *and*. (Chart 9-4)

Directions: Complete the sentences with AUXILIARY VERBS.

1. I **like** rock music, and my roommate _____*does*_____ too.

2. My son **enjoys** monster movies, but I _____.

3. Paul **can't speak** Spanish, and Larry _____ either.

4. My neighbor **walks** to work every morning, but I _____.

5. Carl **can touch** his nose with his tongue, but most people _____.

6. I **am** exhausted from the long trip, and my mother _____ too.

7. I **don't have** a dimple in my chin, but my brother _____.

8. I **visited** the museum yesterday, and my friend _____ too.

9. Water **isn't** solid, but ice _____.

10. Clouds **aren't** solid, and steam _____ either.

◇ PRACTICE 14—SELFSTUDY: Using *too, so, either,* or *neither* after *and*. (Chart 9-5)

Directions: Complete the sentences.

PART I: Complete the sentences with an AUXILIARY + **too** or **either**.

1. Snow **is** white, and clouds _____*are too*_____.

2. I **can't cook,** and my roommate _____*can't either*_____.

3. Squirrels **have** long tails, and cats _____*do too*_____.

4. I **like** movies, and my wife _____.

5. I **don't like** salty food, and my wife _____.

6. Sugar **isn't** expensive, and salt _____.

7. Sugar **is** sweet, and honey _____.

8. Rosa Gomez **wasn't** in class yesterday, and Mr. Nazari _____.

9. Andy **didn't know** the answer to the question, and Tina _____.

10. I **couldn't understand** the substitute teacher, and Yoko _____.

11. Everyone in the room **laughed** at my foolish mistake, and I _____.

12. Fish **can't walk,** and snakes _____.

13. I **like** to fix things around the house, and Ted _____.

14. I'**d rather stay** home this evening, and my husband _____.

PART II: Complete the sentences with **SO** or **NEITHER** + an AUXILIARY.

15. Pasta **is** a famous Italian dish, and _____*so is*_____ pizza.

16. Anteaters **don't have** teeth, and ____*neither do*____ most birds.

17. I **didn't go** to the bank, and _____ my husband.

18. Turtles **are** reptiles, and _____ snakes.

19. My sister **has** dark hair, and _____ I.

20. Gorillas **don't have** tails, and _____ human beings.

21. **I'm studying** English, and _____ Mr. Chu.

22. **I'm not** a native speaker of English, and _____ Mr. Chu.

23. Wood **burns**, and _____ paper.

24. Mountain climbing **is** dangerous, and _____ auto racing.

25. I've **never seen** a monkey in the wild, and _____ my children.

26. When we heard the hurricane warning, I **nailed** boards over my windows and _____ all of my neighbors.

27. My brother and I studied chemistry together. I **didn't pass** the course, and _____ he.

28. Ostriches **can't fly**, and _____ penguins.

◇ PRACTICE 15—GUIDED STUDY: Using *so* or *neither* to respond. (Chart 9-5)

Directions: Pair up with another student (or friend, roommate, etc.).

STUDENT A: With your book open, say the given sentence. Complete the sentence with your own words if necessary.

STUDENT B: Respond to A's statement by using **SO** or **NEITHER**. Your book is closed.

Example: I'm confused.
STUDENT A: *I'm confused.*
STUDENT B: *So am I.*★

─────────────

★This exercise is designed to practice the use of ***so*** and ***neither*** in conversational responses. If, however, STUDENT B doesn't want to agree with, echo, or support STUDENT A's statement, there are alternative responses. For example:

STUDENT A: I'm confused.
STUDENT B: **You are? What's the matter?**
STUDENT A: Frogs don't have tails.
STUDENT B: **Really? Is that so? Hmmmm. I didn't know know that. Are you sure?**
STUDENT A: Ivar's Seafood Restaurant is a good place to eat in Seattle.
STUDENT B: **Oh? I've never eaten there.**

Example: Frogs don't have tails.

STUDENT A: *Frogs don't have tails.*
STUDENT B: *Neither do human beings.*

Example: (Name of a restaurant) is a good place to eat in (this city).

STUDENT A: *Ivar's Seafood Restaurant is a good place to eat in Seattle.*
STUDENT B: *So is Hong Kong Gardens.*

1. I'm thirsty.
2. I'd like (a kind of drink).
3. I studied last night.
4. I study grammar every day.
5. I've never been in (name of a country).
6. I don't like (a kind of food).
7. . . . is a (big/small) country.
8. (Name of a student) is from (name of a country).
9. Soccer is . . . .
10. (Name of a student) has (dark/red/black/etc.) hair.
11. I like (a kind of) weather.
12. Monkeys climb trees.
13. Ice is cold.
14. (. . .) has a part in her/his hair.
15. (name of a country) is a large country.

Directions: Switch roles.

16. I (write/don't write) a lot of letters.
17. I (get/don't get) a lot of mail.
18. San Francisco is a seaport.
19. Fish live in water.
20. I've never seen an iceberg.
21. Swimming is an Olympic sport.
22. I (like/don't like) the weather today.
23. I'd rather go to (name of a place) than (name of a place).
24. (name of a city) is in South America.
25. Oxygen is colorless.
26. Elephants are big animals.
27. (name of a country) is in Africa.
28. I've never had caviar* (OR name of another exotic food) for breakfast.
29. Denmark has no volcanoes.
30. I don't have (red/gray/white) hair.

Caviar = fish eggs (an expensive delicacy in some cultures).

◇ PRACTICE 16—GUIDED STUDY: Using *too, so, either, or neither.* (Chart 9-5)

Directions: Create dialogues (either with a partner or in writing) between A and B. STUDENT A uses the given verb to make a statement (not a question). STUDENT B reacts to A's idea by using **TOO, SO, EITHER,** or **NEITHER** in a response.

Example: would like
STUDENT A: *I'd like to sail around the world someday.*
STUDENT B: *So would I.*   OR   *I would too.* *

Example: didn't want
STUDENT A: *Toshi didn't want to give a speech in front of the class.*
STUDENT B: *Neither did Ingrid.*   OR   *Ingrid didn't either.* *

1. don't have	7. can fly
2. can't speak	8. would like
3. enjoy	9. didn't go
4. isn't going to be	10. are
5. haven't ever seen	11. is sitting
6. will be	12. wasn't

◇ PRACTICE 17—SELFSTUDY: Adverb clauses with *because.* (Chart 9-6)

Directions: <u>Underline</u> the ADVERB CLAUSES. Find the SUBJECT (**S**) and VERB (**V**) of the adverb clause.

                                             S   V
1. Johnny was late for work <u>because [he] [missed] the bus.</u>

2. I closed the door because the room was cold.

3. Because I lost my umbrella, I got wet on the way home.

4. Joe didn't bring his book to class because he couldn't find it.

◇ PRACTICE 18—SELFSTUDY: Adverb clauses with *because.* (Chart 9-6)

Directions: Add PERIODS, COMMAS, and CAPITAL LETTERS as necessary.

1. I opened the window because the room was hot we felt more comfortable then.

    → *I opened the window because the room was hot.* **W***e felt more comfortable then.*

2. I can't use my bicycle because it has a flat tire. → *(no change)*

3. Because his coffee was cold Jack didn't finish it he left it on the table and walked away.

    → *Because his coffee was cold, Jack didn't finish it.* **H***e left it on the table and walked away.*

---

*This practice asks you to use **too, so, either** or **neither** in conversational responses. Other responses are, of course, possible. For example:
   A: I'd like to sail around the world someday.
   B: **Really? Why?**
   A: Toshi didn't want to give a speech in front of the class.
   B: **Oh? Why not?**

4. Annie is very young because she is afraid of the dark she likes to have a light on in her bedroom at night.

5. My sister went to a doctor because she hurt her right knee.

6. Marilyn has a cold because she's not feeling well today she's not going to go to her office.

◇ PRACTICE 19—GUIDED STUDY: Adverb clauses with *because*. (Chart 9-6)

Directions: Add PERIODS, COMMAS, and CAPITAL LETTERS as necessary.

1. Because the weather was bad we canceled our trip into the city we stayed home and watched TV.

2. Mark is an intelligent and ambitious young man because he hopes to get a good job later in life he is working hard to get a good education now.

3. Many species of birds fly to warm climates in the winter because they can't tolerate cold weather.

4. Frank put his head in his hands he was angry and upset because he had lost a lot of work on his computer.

◇ PRACTICE 20—SELFSTUDY: *Because* vs. *so*. (Charts 9-3 and 9-6)

Directions: Give sentences with the same meaning. Use COMMAS as appropriate.

PART I: Restate the sentence, using **SO**.

1. Jack lost his job because he never showed up for work on time.
   → *Jack never showed up for work on time, so he lost his job.*

2. Because I was sleepy, I took a nap.

3. I opened the window because the room was hot.

4. Because it was raining, I stayed indoors.

PART II: Restate the sentence, using **BECAUSE.**

5. Jason was hungry, so he ate.
   → *Because Jason was hungry, he ate.*   OR   *Jason ate because he was hungry.*

6. I was tired, so I went to bed.

7 The water in the river is polluted, so we can't go swimming.

8. My watch is broken, so I was late for my job interview.

Directions: Complete the sentences with your own words.

Example: My friend and I didn't . . . because . . . .
→ ***My friend and I didn't*** *go to the party* ***because*** *we didn't know anyone who was going to be there.*

1. Because I . . . , I . . . .
2. Sometimes people . . . because they . . . .
3. Parents . . . because . . . .
4. Because my parents . . . , ...
5. . . . had a problem. He couldn't . . . because . . . .
6. Because cats . . . , ...
7. My friend . . . yesterday. He didn't . . . because . . . .
8. Because . . . and . . . , they . . . .

◇ PRACTICE 22—SELFSTUDY: Using *because* and *even though*. (Charts 9-6 and 9-7)

Directions: Choose the correct completion.

1. Even though I was hungry, I __**B**__ a lot at dinner.
   A. ate   B. didn't eat

2. Because I was hungry, I _____ a lot at dinner.
   A. ate   B. didn't eat

3. Because I was cold, I _____ my coat.
   A. put on   B. didn't put on

4. Even though I was cold, I _____ my coat.
   A. put on   B. didn't put on

5. Even though Mike _____ sleepy, he stayed up to watch the end of the game on TV.
   A. was   B. wasn't

6. Because Linda _____ sleepy, she went to bed.
   A. was   B. wasn't

7. Because Kate ran too slowly, she _____ the race.
   A. won   B. didn't win

8. Even though Jessica ran fast, she _____ the race.
   A. won   B. didn't win

9. I _____ the test for my driver's license because I wasn't prepared.
   A. failed   B. didn't fail

10. I went to my daughter's school play because she _____ me to be there.
    A. wanted   B. didn't want

11. I bought a new suit for the business trip even though I _____ it.
    A. could afford B. couldn't afford

12. Even though I had a broken leg, I _____ to the conference in New York.
    A. went   B. didn't go

◇ PRACTICE 23—SELFSTUDY: Using *even though* and *although*. (Chart 9-7)

Directions: Choose the best completion.

1. Even though ostriches have wings, __C__.
   A. their feathers are large
   B. they are big birds
   C. they can't fly

2. Although _____, the hungry man ate every bit of it.
   A. an apple is both nutritious and delicious
   B. the cheese tasted good to him
   C. the bread was old and stale

3. The nurse didn't bring Mr. Hill a glass of water even though _____.
   A. she was very busy
   B. she forgot
   C. he asked her three times

4. Although _____, Eric got on the plane.
   A. he is married
   B. he is afraid of flying
   C. the flight attendant welcomed him aboard

5. Even though I looked in every pocket and every drawer, _____.
   A. my keys were under the bed
   B. my roommate helped me look for my keys
   C. I never found my keys

◇ PRACTICE 24—SELFSTUDY: Using *even though/although* and *because*.
                        (Charts 9-6 and 9-7)

Directions: Choose the best completion.

1. It was a hot summer night. We went inside and shut the windows because _____.
   A. the rain stopped
   B. we were enjoying the cool breeze
   C. a storm was coming

2. Cats can't see red even though _____.
   A. it's a bright color
   B. many people like to wear that color
   C. many flowers are bright red

3. Although _____ , my daughter and her friends went swimming in the lake.
   A. it was cold outside
   B. they love to play in the water
   C. the water was warm

4. Because _____ , I joined my daughter and her friends in the lake.
   A. I don't know how to swim
   B. I like to swim
   C. it was cold outside

5. My partner and I worked late into the evening. Even though _____ , we stopped at our favorite restaurant before we went home.
   A. we were very hungry
   B. we were very polite
   C. we were very tired

◇ PRACTICE 25—GUIDED STUDY: Using *even though/although* and *because*.
(Charts 9-6 and 9-7)

Directions: Choose the best completion.

Example: I gave him the money because __**C**__.
   A. I didn't have any
   B. he had a lot of money
   C. I owed it to him

1. My brother came to my graduation ceremony although _____.
   A. he was sick
   B. he was eager to see everyone
   C. he was happy for me

2. Jack hadn't heard or read about the murder even though _____.
   A. he was the murderer
   B. it was on the front page of every newspaper
   C. he was out of town when it occurred

3. We can see the light from an airplane high in the sky at night before we can hear the plane because _____.
   A. light travels faster than sound
   B. airplanes travel at high speeds
   C. our eyes work better than our ears at night

4. Although _____ , he finished the race in first place.
   A. John was full of energy and strength
   B. John was leading all the way
   C. John was far behind in the beginning

5. Snakes don't have ears, but they are very sensitive to vibrations that result from noise. Snakes can sense the presence of a moving object even though _____.
   A. they have ears
   B. they feel vibrations
   C. they can't hear

6. In mountainous areas, melting snow in the spring runs downhill into streams and rivers. The water carries with it sediment, that is, small particles of soil and rock. In the spring, mountain rivers become cloudy rather than clear because _____.
    A. mountain tops are covered with snow
    B. the water from melting snow brings sediment to the river
    C. ice is frozen water

7. Foxes can use their noses to find their dinners because _____.
    A. they have a keen sense of smell
    B. mice and other small rodents move very quickly
    C. they have keen vision

8. When she heard the loud crash, Marge ran outside in the snow although _____.
    A. her mother ran out with her
    B. she wasn't wearing any shoes
    C. she ran as fast as she could

9. Even though his shoes were wet and muddy, Brian _____.
    A. took them off at the front door
    B. walked right into the house and across the carpet
    C. wore wool socks

10. Robert ate dinner with us at our home last night. Although _____, he left right after dinner.
    A. he washed the dishes
    B. there was a good movie at the local theater
    C. I expected him to stay and help with the dishes

11. Alex boarded the bus in front of his hotel. He was on his way to the art museum. Because he _____, he asked the bus driver to tell him where to get off.
    A. was late for work and didn't want his boss to get mad
    B. was carrying a heavy suitcase
    C. was a tourist and didn't know the city streets very well

12. When I attended my first business conference out of town, I felt very uncomfortable during the social events because _____.
      A. we were all having a good time
      B. I didn't know anyone there
      C. I am very knowledgeable in my field

◇ PRACTICE 26—GUIDED STUDY: Punctuating with commas and periods.
                               (Charts 9-1→ 9-7)

Directions: Add COMMAS, PERIODS, and CAPITAL LETTERS as necessary. (There are four adverb clauses in the following passage. Can you find and <u>underline</u> them?)

(1) What is the most common substance on earth? I*i*t isn't wood**,** iron**,** or sand**.** T*t*he most common substance on earth is water it occupies more than seventy percent of the earth's surface it is in lakes rivers and oceans it is in the ground and in the air it is practically everywhere.

(2) Water is vital because life on earth could not exist without it people animals and plants all need water in order to exist every living thing is mostly water a person's body is about sixty-seven percent water a bird is about seventy-five percent water most fruit is about ninety percent water.

(3) Most of the water in the world is saltwater ninety-seven percent of the water on earth is in the oceans because seawater is salty people cannot drink it or use it to grow plants for food only three percent of the earth's water is fresh only one percent of the water in the world is easily available for human use.

(4) Even though water is essential to life human beings often poison it with chemicals from industry and agriculture when people foul water with pollution the quality of all life—plant life animal life and human life—diminishes life cannot exist without fresh water so it is essential for people to take care of this important resource.

◇ PRACTICE 27—SELFSTUDY: Separable vs. nonseparable. (Charts 9-8 and 9-9)

Directions: If the given phrasal verb is separable, mark SEPARABLE. If it is inseparable, mark INSEPARABLE.

1.	CORRECT: I *turned* the light *on.* CORRECT: I *turned on* the light.	*turn on* =	☒ SEPARABLE ☐ NONSEPARABLE
2.	CORRECT: I *ran into* Mary. (INCORRECT: I *ran* Mary *into.)*	*run into* =	☐ SEPARABLE ☒ NONSEPARABLE

3.	CORRECT: Joe *looked up* the definition. CORRECT: Joe *looked* the definition *up*.	*look up* =	☐ SEPARABLE ☐ NONSEPARABLE
4.	CORRECT: I *got off* the bus. (INCORRECT: I *got* the bus *off*.)	*get off* =	☐ SEPARABLE ☐ NONSEPARABLE
5.	CORRECT: I *took off* my coat. CORRECT: I *took* my coat *off*	*take off* =	☐ SEPARABLE ☐ NONSEPARABLE
6.	CORRECT: I *got in* the car and left. (INCORRECT: I *got* the car *in* and left.)	*get in* =	☐ SEPARABLE ☐ NONSEPARABLE
7.	CORRECT: I *figured out* the answer. CORRECT: I *figured* the answer *out*.	*figure out* =	☐ SEPARABLE ☐ NONSEPARABLE
8.	CORRECT: I *turned* the radio *off*. CORRECT: I *turned off* the radio.	*turn off* =	☐ SEPARABLE ☐ NONSEPARABLE

◇ PRACTICE 28—SELFSTUDY: Identifying phrasal verbs. (Charts 9-8 and 9-9)

Directions: <u>Underline</u> the second part of the phrasal verb in each sentence.

1. I *figured* the answer <u>out</u>.

2. The teacher *called* <u>on</u> me in class.

3. I *made* up a story about my childhood.

4. I feel okay now. I *got* over my cold last week.

5. The students *handed* their papers in at the end of the test.

6. I *woke* my roommate up when I got home.

7. I *picked* up a book and started to read.

8. I *turned* the radio on to listen to some music.

9. When I don't know how to spell a word, I *look* it up in the dictionary.

10. I opened the telephone directory and *looked* up the number of a plumber.

11. I *put* my book down and *turned* off the light.

◇ PRACTICE 29—SELFSTUDY: Using phrasal verbs (separable). (Chart 9-8)

Directions: Complete the sentences with the words in the following list.

away	*off*	*out*
down	*on*	*up*
in		

1. I'd like to listen to some music. Would you please *turn* the radio _____**on**_____?

2. My husband *makes* _____ bedtime stories for our children.

3. My arms hurt, so I *put* the baby _____ for a minute, but he started crying right away, so I *picked* him _____ again.

4. A: We need a plumber to fix the kitchen sink. Call one today.

   B: I will.

   A: Don't *put* it _____.

   B: I won't. I'll call today. I promise.

5. A: Why are you wearing your new suit?

   B: I just *put* it _____ to see what it looked like.

   A: It looks fine. *Take* it _____ and hang it up before it gets wrinkled.

6. A: I found this notebook in the wastebasket. It's yours, isn't it?

   B: Yes. I *threw* it _____. I don't need it anymore.

   A: Okay. I thought maybe it had fallen in the wastebasket accidentally.

7. A: I need Jan's address again.

   B: I gave you her address just yesterday.

   A: I'm afraid I've lost it. Tell me again, and I'll *write* it _____.

   B: Just a minute. I have to *look* it _____ in my address book.

8. A: You'll never believe what happened in physics class today.

   B: What happened?

   A: We had a big test today. When I first looked it over, I realized that I couldn't *figure* _____ any of the answers. What happened is that he'd *handed* _____ the wrong test. We hadn't covered that material in class yet.

9. A: *Wake* _____! It's six o'clock! Rise and shine!

   B: What are you doing!? *Turn* the light _____ and close the window curtain!

   A: My goodness but we're grumpy this morning. Come on. It's time to get up, dear. You don't want to be late.

◇ PRACTICE 30—SELFSTUDY: Phrasal verbs. (Charts 9-8 and 9-9)

Directions: Complete the sentences with PRONOUNS and PARTICLES. If the phrasal verb is SEPARABLE, circle SEP. If it is NONSEPARABLE, circle NONSEP.

1. I *got over* my cold . → I got _____*over it*_____ .   SEP   (NONSEP)

2. I *made up* the story. → I made _____*it up*_____ .   (SEP)   NONSEP

3. I *put off* my homework. → I put_____ .   SEP   NONSEP

4. I *wrote down* the numbers. → I wrote _____ .   SEP   NONSEP

5. I *ran into* Robert. → I ran _____ .   SEP   NONSEP

6. I *figured* the answer *out.* → I figured _____ .   SEP   NONSEP

7. I *took off* my shoes. → I took_____ .   SEP   NONSEP

8. I *called on* Susan. → I called _____ .   SEP   NONSEP

9. I *turned off* the lights. → I turned _____ .   SEP   NONSEP

10. I *threw away* the newspaper. → I threw_____ .   SEP   NONSEP

◇ PRACTICE 31—SELFSTUDY: Phrasal verbs. (Charts 9-8 and 9-9)

Directions: Complete the sentences with PARTICLES. Include PRONOUNS in the completions if necessary.

1. I had the flu, but I got _____*over it*_____a couple of days ago.

2. I was wearing gloves. I took _____ before I shook hands with Mr. Zabidi.

3. Stacy needed to find the date that India became independent. She looked _____ in the encyclopedia and wrote _____ in her notebook.

4. The job was finished. I didn't need my tools anymore, so I put _____.

5. It looked like rain, so I got my raincoat from the closet and put _____ before I left the apartment.

6. A: Have you seen Dan this morning?

   B: Not this morning. But I ran _____ at the movie last night.

7. A: Janet's car was stolen this morning!

   B: That's incredible! How did it happen?

   A: She had stopped at the store to pick _____ some groceries. When she returned to her car in the parking lot, she was carrying three bags. She put _____ to get her keys out of her purse. At that moment, a man grabbed the keys out of her hand, got _____ her car, started the engine, and drove away.

8. A: Why do you look so worried?

   B: I don't have my homework. My mother threw _____ with the trash this

      morning. If Ms. Anthony calls _____ in class to answer homework

      questions, I'll have to tell her what happened.

   A: She'll never believe your story. She'll think you made _____.

9. A: You're all wet!

   B: I know. A passing truck went through a big puddle and splashed me.

   A: You'd better take those clothes _____ and put _____

      something clean and dry before you go to work.

CHAPTER 10
Gerunds and Infinitives

◇ PRACTICE 1—SELFSTUDY: Identifying gerunds and infinitives. (Charts 10-1 → 10-2)

Directions: Find and <u>underline</u> the gerunds and infinitives in the following sentences. Circle GER for GERUNDS. Circle INF for INFINITIVES.

1. GER (INF)   Ann promised <u>to wait</u> for me.

2. (GER) INF   I kept <u>walking</u> even though I was tired.

3. GER INF   Alex offered to help me.

4. GER INF   Karen finished writing a letter and went to bed.

5. GER INF   Don't forget to call me tomorrow.

6. GER INF   David was afraid of falling and hurting himself.

7. GER INF   Working in a coal mine is a dangerous job.

8. GER INF   It is easy to grow vegetables.

◇ PRACTICE 2—GUIDED STUDY: Verb + gerund. (Chart 10-2)

Directions: Complete the sentences in COLUMN A by using a verb from COLUMN B and your own words. Don't use a verb from COLUMN B more than one time.

Example: I often postpone + write
→ *I often postpone writing thank you notes, and then I have to apologize for sending them late.*

COLUMN A	COLUMN B		
1. I often postpone	A. buy	H. go	O. play
2. I enjoy	B. close	I. help	P. take
3. I'm considering	C. do	J. learn	Q. teach
4. Would you mind	D. eat	K. listen	R. try
5. I finished	E. exercise	L. love	S. watch
6. I'll never stop	F. finish	M. make	T. write
7. Do you ever think about	G. give	N. open	
8. You should keep			
9. Sometimes I put off			

◇ PRACTICE 3—SELFSTUDY: *Go + gerund.* (Chart 10-3)

Directions: Use the given ideas to complete the sentences with a form of **GO** + the appropriate GERUND to describe the activity.

1. I love to dance. Last night, my husband and I danced for hours.

   → Last night, my husband and I ___*went dancing*___.

2. Later this afternoon, Ted is going to take a long walk in the woods.

   → Ted ___*is going to go hiking*___ later today.

3. Yesterday Alice visited many stores and bought some clothes and makeup.

   → Yesterday, Alice _____.

4. Let's go to the beach and jump in the water.

   → Let's _____.

5. My grandfather takes his fishing pole to a farm pond every Sunday.

   → My grandfather _____ every Sunday.

6. When I visit a new city, I like to look around at the sights.

   → When I visit a new city, I like to _____.

7. I love to put up a small tent by a stream, make a fire, and listen to the sounds of the forest through the night.

   → I love to _____.

8. I want to take the sailboat out on the water this afternoon.

   → I want to _____ this afternoon.

9. Once a year, we take our skis to our favorite mountain resort and enjoy an exciting weekend.

   → Once a year, we _____

   at our favorite mountain resort.

10. Last year on my birthday, my friends and I went up in an airplane, put on parachutes, and jumped out of the plane at a very high altitude.

    → Last year, on my birthday, my friends and I

    _____.

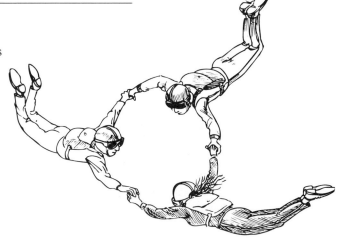

◇ PRACTICE 4—SELFSTUDY: Verb + gerund vs. infinitive. (Charts 10-2 → 10-4)

Directions: Choose the correct completion.

1. I would like __**B**__ you and some of my other friends for dinner sometime.
   A. inviting   B. to invite

2. I enjoyed _____ with my family at the lake last summer.
   A. being   B. to be

3. Don agreed _____ me move out of my apartment this weekend.
   A. helping   B. to help

4. My parents can't afford _____ all of my college expenses.
   A. paying   B. to pay

5. Liang-Siok, would you mind _____ this letter on your way home?
   A. mailing   B. to mail

6. Do you expect _____ this course? If so, you'd better work harder.
   A. passing   B. to pass

7. Adam offered _____ for me tonight because I feel awful.
   A. working   B. to work

8. I refuse _____ your proposal. I've made up my mind.
   A. considering   B. to consider

9. I wish you would consider _____ my proposal. I know I can do the job.
   A. accepting   B. to accept

10. I don't think I'll ever finish _____ this report. It just goes on and on.
    A. writing   B. to write

11. I would enjoy _____ you in Cairo while you're studying there.
    A. visiting   B. to visit

12. The children seem _____ why they have to stay home tonight.
    A. understanding   B. to understand

13. Don't forget _____ all of the doors before you go to bed.
    A. locking   B. to lock

14. I'm really sorry. I didn't mean _____ your feelings.
    A. hurting   B. to hurt

15. Why do you keep _____ me the same question over and over again?
    A. asking   B. to ask

16. I've decided _____ for another job. I'll never be happy here.
    A. looking   B. to look

17. You need _____ harder if you want to get the promotion.
    A. trying   B. to try

18. Why do you pretend _____ his company? I know you don't like him.
    A. enjoying   B. to enjoy

19. Let's get together tonight. I want to talk about _____ a new business.
    A. opening   B. to open

20. I have a secret. Do you promise _____ no one?
    A. telling   B. to tell

21. The president plans _____ everyone a bonus at the end of the year.
    A. giving   B. to give

22. I have a good job, and I hope _____ myself all through school.
    A. supporting   B. to support

23. I can't wait _____ work today. I'm taking off on vacation tonight.
    A. finishing   B. to finish

24. My neighbor and I get up at six every morning and go _____.
    A. jogging   B. to jog

◇ PRACTICE 5—SELFSTUDY: Verb + gerund or infinitive. (Charts 10-2 → 10-5)

   Directions: Choose the correct answer or answers. **Both answers may be correct.**

   1. I want _____**B**_____ the comedy special on TV tonight.
      A. watching   B. to watch

   2. I'm a people-watcher. I like _____**A, B**_____ people in public places.
      A. watching   B. to watch

   3. I've already begun _____ ideas for my new novel.
      A. collecting   B. to collect

   4. A group of Chinese scientists plan _____ their discovery at the world conference next
      spring.
      A. presenting   B. to present

   5. Every time I wash my car, it starts _____.
      A. raining   B. to rain

   6. Angela and I continued _____ for several hours.
      A. talking   B. to talk

   7. I love _____ on the beach during a storm.
      A. walking   B. to walk

   8. I would love _____ a walk today.
      A. taking   B. to take

9. Are you sure you don't mind _____ Johnny for me while I go to the store?
   A. watching   B. to watch

10. Annie hates _____ in the rain.
    A. driving   B. to drive

11. My roommate can't stand _____ to really loud rock music.
    A. listening   B. to listen

12. I don't like _____ in front of other people.
    A. singing   B. to sing

13. Would you like _____ to the concert with us?
    A. going   B. to go

14. Most children can't wait _____ their presents on their birthday.
    A. opening   B. to open

◇ PRACTICE 6—GUIDED STUDY: Verb + gerund or infinitive. (Chart 10-5)

Directions: In writing, or orally in small groups, discuss what you like and don't like to do. Use the given ideas to make sentences that begin with:

I like	*I don't like*	*I don't mind*
I love	*I hate*	
I enjoy	*I can't stand*	

1. cook
   → *I like to cook | I like cooking | I hate to cook | I hate cooking | I don't mind cooking.*

2. live in this city

3. wash dishes

4. fly

5. wait in airports

6. read novels in my spare time

7. eat a delicious meal slowly

8. drive on city streets during rush hour

9. speak in front of a large group

10. play cards for money

11. go to parties where I don't know a single person

12. listen to the sounds of the city while I'm trying to get to sleep

13. visit with friends I haven't seen in a long time

14. get in between two friends who are having an argument

15. travel to strange and exotic places

◇ PRACTICE 7—GUIDED STUDY: Gerunds vs. infinitives. (Charts 10-1 → 10-5)

Directions: Complete the sentences with the correct form, GERUND or INFINITIVE, of the words in parentheses.

A: Have you made any vacation plans?

B: I was hoping *(1. go)* _____**to go**_____ to an island off the Atlantic coast, but my wife

wanted *(2. drive)* _____ down the Pacific coast. We've decided

(3. compromise) _____ by going to neither coast. We've agreed *(4. find)*

_____ a place where both of us want *(5. go)* _____.

A: So where are you going?

B: Well, we've been considering *(6. go)* _____ *(7. fish)* _____

in Canada. We've also discussed *(8. take)* _____ a train across central and

western Canada. We also have been talking about *(9. rent)* _____

a sailboat and *(10. go)* _____ *(11. sail)* _____

in the Gulf of Mexico.

A: Have you ever thought about *(12. stay)* _____ home and *(13. relax)*

_____?

B: That's not a vacation to me. If I stay home during my vacation, I always end up doing all the

chores around home that I've put off *(14. do)* _____ for the past year. When

I go on a holiday, I like *(15. visit)* _____ new places and *(16. do)*

_____ new things. I enjoy *(17. see)* _____ parts of the

world I've never seen before.

A: What place would you like *(18. visit)* _____ the most?

B: I'd love *(19. go)* _____ *(20. camp)* _____ in New Zealand.

My wife loves *(21. camp)* _____ in new places too, but I'm afraid she might

refuse *(22. go)* _____ to New Zealand. She doesn't like long plane flights.

A: Why don't you just pick a spot on a map? Then call and make a hotel reservation.

B: Neither of us can stand *(23. spend)* _____ two whole weeks at a luxury hotel

somewhere. I don't mean *(24. say)* _____ anything bad about big hotels, but

both of us seem *(25. like)* _____ more adventurous vacations.

A: Well, keep *(26. think)* _____ about it. I'm sure you'll figure out a really great

place for your vacation.

B: We'll have to stop *(27. think)* _____ about it sometime soon and make a

decision.

B: I can't wait *(28. find)* _____ out where you decide *(29. go)*

_____ . I'll expect *(30. hear)* _____ from you when you

make a decision. Don't forget *(31. call)* _____ me.

A: Hmmm. Maybe we should go *(32. ski)* _____ in Switzerland. Or perhaps

we could go *(33. water-ski)* _____ on the Nile. Then there's the possibility

of going *(34. hike)* _____ in the Andes. Of course, we'd probably enjoy

(35. swim) _____ off the Great Barrier Reef of Australia. And we shouldn't

postpone *(36. explore)* _____ the Brazilian rain forest much longer.

Someday I'd really like *(37. climb)* _____ to the top of an active volcano and

(38. look) _____ inside the crater. Or maybe we could . . . .

◇ PRACTICE 8—SELFSTUDY: Uncompleted infinitives. (Chart 10-6)

Directions: Cross out the unnecessary words in Speaker B's responses.

1. A: Did you pay the electric bill?
   B: Not yet. But I'm going to ~~pay the electric bill~~.

2. A: Why didn't you go to class this morning?
   B: I didn't want to go to class this morning.

3. A: Did you call your mother?
   B: No, but I ought to call my mother.

4. A: Have you taken your vacation yet this year?
   B: No, I haven't, but I intend to take my vacation.

Directions: Complete the dialogues with your own words. Then explain the full meaning of the uncompleted infinitives.

1. A: Would you like___*to go to a movie with us tonight*_____?

    B: I'd love to!   (→ *I'd love to go to a movie with you tonight.*)

2. A: Does _____*Yoko*_____enjoy _____*meeting new people*_____?

    B: She seems to.   (→ *She seems to enjoy meeting new people.*)

3. A: Did you _____?

    B: No.

    A: Well, you ought to.

4. A: Why didn't _____?

    B: I didn't want to.

5. A: Would you like to _____?

    B: Yes, but I can't afford to.

6. A: Do you _____?

    B: No, but I used to.

7. A: You should _____.

    B: I intend to.

8. A: I'm not going _____.

    B: But you have to!

9. A: Have you _____?

    B: Not yet, but I'm planning to.

10. A: _____?

    B: I'd really like to, but I can't.

◇ PRACTICE 10—SELFSTUDY: Preposition + gerund. (Chart 10-7 and Appendix 1)

Directions: Using the verbs in parentheses, complete the sentences with PREPOSITIONS and GERUNDS. Refer to the list of expressions with prepositions at the bottom of the page if necessary.*

1. I believe _____*in telling*_____ the truth no matter what. *(tell)*

2. I wish the weather would get better. I'm tired _____*of having to be*_____ inside all the time.

    (have to be)

---

*EXPRESSIONS WITH PREPOSITIONS:

be afraid of	*be* good at	plan on
apologize for	have the (bad) habit of	*be* responsible for
believe in	*be* in danger of	stop someone from
concentrate on	*be* in the habit of	succeed in
dream about	insist on	talk into doing
be excited about	*be* interested in	thank someone for
feel like	look forward to	*be* tired of
forgive someone for	*be* nervous about	worry about

3. I don't go swimming because I'm afraid _____. (drown)

4. Greg is nervous _____ his girlfriend's parents for the first time. (meet)

5. I don't know how to thank you _____ me. (help)

6. Are you interested _____ to a bullfight? (go)

7. I worked on it all night, but I didn't succeed _____ the problem. (solve)

8. I just can't get excited _____ Disneyland for the third time in two years. (visit)

9. Carlos has the irritating habit _____ gum very loudly. (chew)

10. Why do you constantly worry _____ your parents? (please)

11. Jonathan! Please concentrate _____ your assignment. (read)

12. Every summer, I look forward _____ a vacation with my family. (take)

13. Do you feel _____ me why you're so sad? (tell)

14. I apologize _____, but I was trying to protect you from the truth. Sometimes the truth hurts. (lie)

15. Why do you always insist _____ for everything when we go out for dinner? (pay)

16. I'm in the habit _____ every morning, but I'm too tired today. (jog)

17. I want you to know that I'm sorry. I don't know if you can ever forgive me _____ you so much trouble. (cause)

18. I'm not very good _____ names. (remember)

19. I'm not happy in my work. I often dream _____ my job. (quit)

20. How do you stop someone _____ something you know is wrong? (do)

21. You can't convince me to change my mind. After what she did, you'll never talk me _____ her. (forgive)

22. I'm too tired to cook, but I hadn't planned _____ out tonight. (eat)

23. Who's responsible _____ these coffee beans all over the floor? (spill)

24. You'd better be careful. You're in danger _____ this class. (fail)

25. Anna made a lot of big mistakes at work. That's why she was afraid _____ her job. (lose)*

---

*Note that *lose* is spelled with one "o." The word *loose*, with two "o's," is an adjective meaning "not tight." (e.g., My shirt is big and loose.) Pronunciation difference: *lose* = /luwz/; *loose* = /luws/.

◇ PRACTICE 11—GUIDED STUDY: Preposition + gerund. (Chart 10-7 and Appendix 1)

Directions: In writing or in groups, make up sentences that contain GERUNDS. Include the appropriate PREPOSITION in each.

Example: apologize to (. . .) + interrupt / be / call
→ *You should apologize to Tarik for interrupting him.*
I apologized to my friend for being late.
Rosa apologized to me for calling after midnight.

1. be nervous + *speak / go / get*
2. thank (. . .) + *open / help / invite*
3. feel like (. . .) + *go / have / take*
4. look forward + *do / stop / skydive*
5. apologize to (. . .) + *sell / give / leave*
6. worry + *lose / not have / be*
7. forgive (. . .) + *lie / take / forget*
8. be excited + *go / meet / move*
9. insist + *answer / drive / fly*
10. believe + *help / tell / trust*

◇ PRACTICE 12—SELFSTUDY: Using *by* + gerund. (Chart 10-8)

Directions: Describe what the people did by using **BY** + a GERUND.

1. *Mary:* How did you comfort the child?
   Sue: I held him in my arms.

   → Sue comforted the child _____**by holding**_____ him in her arms.

2. *Pat:* How did you improve your vocabulary?
   Nadia: I read a lot of books.

   → Nadia improved her vocabulary _____ a lot of books.

3. *Kirk:* How did Grandma amuse the children?
   Sally: She told them a story.

   → Grandma amused the children _____ them a story.

4. *Masako:* How did you improve your English?
   Pedro: I watched TV a lot.

   → Pedro improved his English _____ TV a lot.

5. *Jeffrey:* How did you catch up with the bus?
   Jim: I ran as fast as I could.

   → Jim caught up with the bus _____ as fast as he could.

6. *Sam:* How did you recover from your cold?
   Abdul: I stayed in bed and took care of myself.

   → Abdul recovered _____ in bed and _____
   care of himself.

7. *Mr. Lee:* How did you earn your children's respect?
   Mr. Fox: I treated them with respect at all times.

   → Mr. Smith earned his children's respect _____
   them with respect at all times.

◇ PRACTICE 13—GUIDED STUDY: Using *by* + gerund. (Chart 10-8)

Directions: Complete the sentences in Column A with **BY** + an appropriate idea from Column B

Example: I arrived on time by taking a taxi instead of the bus.

COLUMN A	COLUMN B
1. I arrived on time	A. tighten the loose screws
2. I put out the fire	B. count the rings
3. Giraffes can reach the leaves at the top	C. read the directions on the package
4. I fixed the chair	D. walk on the bottom of the riverbed
5. Sara was able to buy an expensive stereo system	E. pour water on it
6. A hippopotamus can cross a river	F. work all through the night
7. I figured out how to cook the noodles	G. stretch their long necks
8. Pam finished her project on time	H. save her money for two years
9. You can figure out how old a tree is	✔ I. take a taxi instead of a bus

CROSS-SECTION

20 RINGS
20 YEARS OLD

◇ PRACTICE 14—SELFSTUDY: Using *with*. (Chart 10-8)

Directions: Complete the sentences using **WITH** and appropriate words from the following list.

✔*a broom*   *a needle and thread*   *a shovel*
a hammer   *a pair of scissors*   *a spoon*
a key   *a saw*   *a thermometer*
a knife

1. I swept the floor _____**with a broom**_____.

2. I sewed the button on my shirt _____.

3. I cut the wood _____.

4. I took my temperature _____.

5. I stirred my coffee _____.

6. I opened the locked door _____.

7. I dug a hole in the ground _____.

8. I nailed two pieces of wood together _____.

9. I cut the meat _____.

10. I cut the paper _____.

◇ PRACTICE 15—SELFSTUDY: *By* vs. *with*. (Chart 10-8)

Directions: Complete the sentences with **BY** or **WITH**.

1. Alice greeted me _____**with**_____ a smile.

2. Ms. Williams goes to work every day _____**by**_____ bus.

3. I pounded the nail into the wood _____ a hammer.

4. Tom went to the next city _____ train.

5. I got in touch with Bill _____ phone.

6. Akihiko eats _____ chopsticks.

7. I didn't notice that the envelope wasn't addressed to me. I opened it _____ mistake.

8. I sent a message to Ann _____ fax.

9. Jack protected his eyes from the sun _____ his hand.

10. Janice put out the fire _____ a bucket of water.

11. I pay my bills _____ mail.

12. I solved the math problem _____ a calculator.

13. We traveled to Boston _____ car.

14. The rider kicked the sides of the horse _____ her heels.

15. Jim was extremely angry. He hit the wall _____ his fist.

16. At the beach, Julie wrote her name in the sand _____ her finger.

◇ PRACTICE 16—SELFSTUDY: Gerund as subject; *it* + infinitive. (Charts 10-9 → 10-10)

Directions: Complete the sentences by using a GERUND as the subject or IT + INFINITIVE. Add the word IS where appropriate. Use the verbs in the following list.

complete	eat	live
drive	✔ learn	swim

1. a. ___**It is**___ easy for anyone ___**to learn**___ how to cook an egg.

   b. ___**Learning**___ how to cook an egg ___**is**___ easy for anyone.

2. a. _____ nutritious food _____ important for your health.

   b. _____ important for your health _____ nutritious food.

3. a. _____ on the wrong side of the road _____ against the law.

   b. _____ against the law _____ on the wrong side of the road.

4. a. _____ fun for both children and adults _____ in the ocean.

   b. _____ in the ocean _____ fun for both children and adults.

5. a. _____ expensive _____ in a dormitory?

   b. _____ in a dormitory expensive?

6. a. _____ difficult _____ these sentences correctly?

   b. _____ these sentences correctly difficult?

◇ PRACTICE 17—GUIDED STUDY: Gerund as subject; *it* + infinitive. (Chart 10-9)

Directions: Make sentences by combining ideas from Column A and Column B. Use GERUND SUBJECTS or IT + INFINITIVE.

Example: Riding a bicycle is easy / dangerous / fun / relaxing.   OR
It is easy / dangerous / fun / relaxing to ride a bicycle.

COLUMN A

1. ride a bicycle
2. read newspapers
3. study grammar
4. play tennis
5. steal cars
6. listen to a two-hour speech
7. predict the exact time of an earthquake
8. forget someone's name
9. walk alone through a dark forest at night
10. go fishing with your friends
11. know the meaning of every word in a dictionary
12. be honest with yourself at all times
13. change a flat tire
14. visit museums

COLUMN B

A. against the law
B. boring
C. dangerous
D. easy
E. educational
F. embarrassing
G. exciting
H. frightening
I. fun
J. hard
K. important
L. impossible
M. relaxing
N. a waste of time

◇ PRACTICE 18—GUIDED STUDY: *It* + *for* (*someone*) + infinitive. (Chart 10-10)

Directions: Make sentences using IT + FOR (someone) + INFINITIVE by combining ideas from Columns A, B, and C. Add your own words if you wish.

Example: difficult

→   *It is difficult for me to be on time for class.*
It is difficult for some people to learn how to swim.
It's difficult for children to understand adults' behavior.

COLUMN A	COLUMN B	COLUMN C
1. difficult	anyone	spend time with friends
2. easy	children	predict the exact time of an earthquake
3. fun	me	change a flat tire
4. important	most people	be on time for class
5. impossible	some people	understand adults' behavior
6. enjoyable	students	obey their parents
7. interesting		observe animals in their wild habitat
8. possible		visit new places
		learn how to swim
		live on the planet Mars

◇ PRACTICE 19—GUIDED STUDY: *It + take.* (Charts 6-11 and 10-9 → 10-10)

Directions: Use your own words to complete the following sentences.

Example: It takes . . . hours to . . . .
  → **It takes** five **hours to** fly from Los Angeles to Honolulu.

Example: It takes a lot of work for . . . to . . . .
  → **It takes a lot of work for** most small businesses **to** succeed.

1. It takes time for . . . to . . . .
2. It takes a lot of money to . . . .
3. It takes . . . minutes to . . . .
4. How long does it take to . . . ?

5. It will take . . . years for . . . to . . . .
6. It takes patience / courage / skill to . . . .
7. It takes hard work for . . . to . . . .
8. It takes stamina and determination to . . . .

◇ PRACTICE 20—GUIDED STUDY: *It + for (someone) + infinitive.* (Chart 10-10)

Directions: Complete the sentences with your own words.

1. It is easy for . . . to . . . .
2. It's traditional for . . . to . . . .
3. It's impossible for . . . to . . . .
4. It takes *(a length of time)* for . . . to . . . .

5. It's sensible for . . . to . . . .
6. Is it necessary for . . . to . . . ?
7. It's important for . . . to . . . .
8. It's difficult for . . . to . . . .

◇ PRACTICE 21—SELFSTUDY: *(In order) to.* (Chart 10-11)

Directions: Complete the sentences in Column A by using the ideas in Column B. Connect the ideas with (**IN ORDER**) **TO**.

Example: I called the hotel desk (in order) to ask for an extra pillow.

COLUMN A
1. I called the hotel desk
2. I turned on the radio
3. I looked in the encyclopedia
4. People wear boots
5. Andy went to Egypt
6. Ms. Lane stood on tiptoe
7. The dentist moved the light closer to my face
8. I clapped my hands and yelled
9. Maria took a walk in the park
10. I offered my cousin some money

COLUMN B
A. keep their feet warm and dry
B. reach the top shelf
C. listen to a ball game
D. find the population of Malaysia
✔ E. ask for an extra pillow
F. chase a stray dog away
G. help him pay the rent
H. get some fresh air and exercise
I. see the ancient pyramids
J. look into my mouth

◇ PRACTICE 22—SELFSTUDY: Purpose: *to* vs. *for.* (Chart 10-11)

Directions: Complete the sentences with **TO** or **FOR**.

1. Sam went to the hospital _____*for*_____ an operation.

2. I hired a cab _____*to*_____ take me to the boat dock.

3. Frank stayed after school _____ get some extra help from the teacher.

4. I play tennis twice a week _____ exercise and relaxation.

5. I sent a card to Carol _____ wish her a happy birthday.

6. Two police officers came to my apartment _____ ask me about my cousin.

7. Mr. Wong works in his garden _____ the pure pleasure of it.

8. I looked in the encyclopedia _____ information about Ecuador.

9. Jennifer used some medicine _____ cure an infection on her arm.

10. I lent Yvette money _____ her school expenses.

11. My three brothers, two sisters, and parents all came to town _____ attend my graduation.

12. I went to my boss _____ permission to take the rest of the day off.

◇ PRACTICE 23—SELFSTUDY: *Too* and *enough* + infinitive. (Chart 10-12)

Directions: Complete the sentences by choosing from the given words. Use **TOO** or **ENOUGH** and an INFINITIVE.

1. *strong / lift* I'm not _____ ***strong enough to lift*** _____ a refrigerator.

2. *weak / lift* Most people are _____ ***too weak to lift*** _____ a refrigerator without help.

3. *full / hold* My suitcase is _____ any more clothes.

4. *large / hold* My suitcase isn't _____ all the clothes I want to take on my trip.

5. *busy / answer* I was _____ _____ the phone. I let it keep ringing until the caller gave up.

6. *early/get*   We got to the concert _____ good seats.

7. *big/get*   Rex is _____ into Bobo's doghouse.

8. *big/hold*   Julie's purse is _____

_____ her dog Pepper.

◇ PRACTICE 24—SELFSTUDY: *Too* and *enough* + infinitive. (Chart 10-12)

Directions: Complete the sentences with **TOO** or **ENOUGH**. Write a slash (/) if nothing is needed in a blank.

1. Alan is _____ smart _____ to make that kind of mistake.

2. Alan is _____ smart _____ to understand how to solve that

   problem.   *too*   */*

3. My pocket is ___*/*_____ big ___*enough*_____ to hold my wallet. I always carry

   my wallet there.

4. A horse is _____ big _____ for a person to lift.

5. I'm uncomfortable. This room is _____ hot _____. Why don't

   you open the window?

6. That watch is _____ expensive _____. I can't afford it.

7. Are you _____ tall _____ to reach that book for me? The green

   one on the top shelf. Thanks.

8. Ask John to help you move that box. He's _____ strong _____ to lift it.

9. I am _____ busy _____ to help you right now.

10. I think this problem is _____ important _____ to require our immediate attention.

11. Nora is not _____ tired _____ to finish the project before she goes home.

12. Our company is _____ successful _____ to start several new branches overseas.

◇ PRACTICE 25—SELFSTUDY: Gerunds vs. infinitives. (Charts 10-1 → 10-10)

Directions: Complete the sentences with the words in parentheses: GERUND or INFINITIVE.

1. It's difficult for me *(remember)* ___**to remember**___ phone numbers.

2. My cat is good at *(catch)* ___**catching**___ mice.

3. I bought a newspaper *(look)* _____ at the ads for apartments for rent.

4. Tourists like *(go)* _____ *(swim)* _____ in the warm ocean in Hawaii.

5. I called my friend *(invite)* _____ her for dinner.

6. Hillary talked about *(go)* _____ to graduate school.

7. Sarosh found out what was happening by *(listen)* _____ carefully to everything that was said.

8. Children, stop *(draw)* _____ pictures on the tablecloth!

9. Professor Amani has a strong accent. It is difficult for his students *(understand)* _____ him. He needs *(improve)* _____ his pronunciation if he wants *(be)* _____ a good lecturer. *(lecture)* _____ requires good communication skills.

10. A: Hi! I'm home!

    B: Welcome back. Did you have a good trip?

    A: Yes, thanks. How's everything? How are my goldfish? I hope you didn't forget *(feed)* _____ them.

    B: Oh, my gosh!

11. Dan's goldfish died when he was away on a trip because his roommate forgot *(feed)* _____ them. Dan is considering *(get)* _____ a new roommate.

12. My friend Akihiko has goldfish in a pond in his garden. He enjoys *(feed)* _____
   them one by one with chopsticks.

13. Michelle Yin Yin Ko works sixteen hours a day *(earn)* _____ enough
   money *(take)* _____ care of her elderly parents as well as her three
   children.

14. It takes care, patience, and a little luck *(take)* _____ a really good
   photograph of wildlife.

15. No matter how wonderful a trip is, it's always good *(get)* _____ back
   home and *(sleep)* _____ in one's own bed.

16. A: Quit *(stare)* _____ at the phone. Greg isn't going to call.

   B: I keep *(think)* _____ the phone will ring any second.

   A: I don't mean *(be)* _____ unsympathetic, but I think you'd better
      forget about Greg. It's over.

17. It's important to your health for you *(work)* _____ at a job you like.
   If you hate *(go)* _____ to your job, you should seriously think about
   (look) _____ for a different kind of job. The stress of *(do)*
   _____ work you hate day in and day out can damage your health.

◇ PRACTICE 26—SELFSTUDY: Gerunds vs. infinitives. (Chart 10-1 → 10-10)

   Directions: Find and <u>underline</u> the GERUNDS and INFINITIVES in the following.

   1. Jim offered <u>to help</u> me with my work.
   2. My son isn't old enough to stay home alone.
   3. Do you enjoy being alone sometimes, or do you prefer to be with other people all the time?
   4. I called my friend to thank her for the lovely gift.
   5. Mary talked about going downtown tomorrow, but I'd like to stay home.
   6. It is interesting to learn about earthquakes.
   7. Approximately one million earthquakes occur around the world in a year's time. Six thousand
      can be felt by humans. Of those, one hundred and twenty are strong enough to cause serious
      damage to buildings, and twenty are violent enough to destroy a city.
   8. It's important to respect the power of nature. A recent earthquake destroyed a bridge in
      California. It took five years for humans to build the bridge. It took nature fifteen seconds to
      knock it down.

9. Predicting earthquakes is difficult. I read about one scientist who tries to predict earthquakes by reading the daily newspaper's lost-and-found ads for lost pets. He believes that animals can sense an earthquake before it comes. He thinks they then begin to act strangely. Dogs and cats respond to the threat by running away to a safer place. By counting the number of ads for lost pets, he expects to be able to predict when an earthquake will occur.

◇ PRACTICE 27—GUIDED STUDY: Gerunds vs. infinitives. (Charts 10-1 → 10-10)

Directions: Complete the sentences with the words in parentheses: GERUND or INFINITIVE.

1. (study) _____**Studying**_____ English is fun.

2. My boss makes a habit of (jot)* _____ quick notes to her employees when they've done a good job.

3. From the earth, the sun and the moon appear (be) _____ almost the same size.

4. A: I don't like airplanes.

    B: Why? Are you afraid of (fly) _____ ?

    A: No, I'm afraid of (crash) _____ .

5. I keep (forget) _____ (call) _____ my friend Louise. I'd better write myself a note.

6. People in the modern world are wasteful of natural resources. For example, every three months, people in North America throw away enough aluminum (build) _____ an entire airplane.

7. I am so busy! I have just enough time (do) _____ what I need (do) _____ , but not enough time (do) _____ what I'd like (do) _____ .

8. (ask) _____ others about themselves and their lives is one of the secrets of (get) _____ along with other people. If you want (make) _____ and (keep) _____ friends, it is important (be) _____ sincerely interested in other people's lives.

9. A: Have you called Amanda yet?

    B: No. I keep (put) _____ it off.

    A: Why?

_____
*Jot = write quickly and briefly.

B: She's mad at me for *(forget)* _____ *(send)* _____ a

card on her birthday.

A: It's silly for her *(get)* _____ mad about something like that. Just call her

and say you are sorry about *(remember, not)* _____ to wish

her a happy birthday. She can't stay mad at you forever.

10. In days of old, it was customary for a servant *(taste)* _____ the king's food

before the king ate *(make)* _____ sure it was not poisoned.

11. One of my good friends, Larry, has the bad habit of *(interrupt)* _____

others while they're talking.

12. I like *(travel)* _____ to out-of-the-way places. I don't like *(go)*

_____ to usual tourist places when I'm on holiday.

13. Large bee colonies have 80,000 workers. These worker bees must visit fifty million flowers

(make) _____ one kilogram (2.2 pounds) of honey. It's no wonder that

"busy as a bee" is a common expression.

14. Exercise is good for you. Why don't you walk up the stairs instead of *(take)*

_____ the elevator?

15. Stop *(crack)* _____ those nuts with your teeth! Here. Use a nutcracker.

Do you want *(be)* _____ toothless by the time you're thirty?

Directions: Complete the sentences with the words in parentheses: GERUND or INFINITIVE.

1. A: Let's quit *(argue)* _____ **arguing** _____. We're getting nowhere. Let's just agree

   (disagree) _____ and still *(be)* _____ friends.

   B: Sounds good to me. And I apologize for *(raise)* _____ my voice. I

   didn't mean *(yell)* _____ at you.

   A: That's okay. I didn't intend *(get)* _____ angry at you either.

2. A: David, why did you want *(sneak)* _____ into the movie theater without

   (pay) _____?

   B: I don't know, Mom. My friends talked me into *(do)* _____ it, I guess.

   A: That's not a very good reason. You are responsible for your actions, not your friends.

   B: I know. I'm sorry.

   A: How does this make you feel? Do you like yourself for *(try)* _____

   (sneak) _____ into the theater?

   B: No. It doesn't make me feel good about myself.

   A: You're young. We all have lessons like this to learn as we grow up. Just remember: It's

   essential for you *(have)* _____ a good opinion of yourself. It's very

   important for all of us *(like)* _____ ourselves. When we do something

   wrong, we stop *(like)* _____ ourselves, and that doesn't feel good. Do

   you promise never *(do)* _____ anything like that again?

   B: Yes. I promise! I'm really sorry, Mom.

3. Different cultures have different gestures. When North Americans meet someone, they usually

   offer a strong handshake and look the other person straight in the eye. In some countries,

   however, it is impolite *(shake)* _____ hands firmly, and *(look)*

   _____ the person in the eye is equally rude.

4. How close do you stand to another person when you are speaking? North Americans prefer

   (stand) _____ just a little less than an arm's length from someone. Many

   people in the Middle East and Latin America prefer *(move)* _____ in

   closer than that during a conversation.

5. *(Smile)* _____ at another person is a universal, cross-cultural gesture.

   Everyone throughout the world understands the meaning of a smile.

6. A: What do you feel like *(do)* _____ this afternoon?

   B: I feel like *(go)* _____ *(shop)* _____ at the mall.

   A: I feel like *(go)* _____ to a used car lot and *(pretend)*

   _____ *(be)* _____ interested in *(buy)*

   _____ a car.

   B: You're kidding. Why would you want *(do)* _____ that?

   A: I like cars. Maybe we could even take one out for a test drive. You know I'm planning *(get)*

   _____ a car as soon as I can afford *(buy)* _____

   one. I can't wait *(have)* _____ my own car. Maybe we'll find the car

   of my dreams at a used car lot. Come on. It sounds like fun.

   B: Nah. Not me. You go ahead. *(pretend)* _____ *(be)*

   _____ interested in *(buy)* _____ a used car

   doesn't sound like my idea of fun.

◇ PRACTICE 29—SELFSTUDY: Phrasal verbs (separable). (Chart 10-13)

   Directions: Complete the sentences with the correct PARTICLE from the list below.

   away   *back*   *down*   *off*   *on*   *out*   *up*

   1. When are you going to *pay* me _____**back**_____ the money you owe me?

   2. *Turn* _____ the radio! It's too loud! I can't hear myself think.

   3. Debra *put* _____ the fire in the wastebasket with a fire extinguisher.

   4. After I wash and dry the dishes, I *put* them _____. In other words, I put them in the

   cupboard where they belong.

   5. Before you buy shoes, you should *try* them _____ to see if they fit.

   6. I can't hear the TV. Could you please *turn* it _____? Thanks. No, don't *shut* it

   _____! I want to hear the news. I wanted you to make it louder, not turn it off.

   7. A: That's mine! *Give* it _____!

   B: No, it's not. It's mine!

   C: Now children. Don't fight.

   8. A: I don't hear anyone on the other end of the phone.

   B: Just *hang* _____. It's probably a wrong number.

9. A: I hear that Tom *asked* you _____ for next Saturday night.

    B: Yes, he did. He called a couple of hours ago. We're going to the symphony concert.

    A: The concert's been *called* _____. Didn't you hear about it? The musicians are on strike.

    B: No, I didn't. I'd better *call* Tom _____ and ask him what he wants to do.

◇ PRACTICE 30—SELFSTUDY: Phrasal verbs (separable). (Chart 10-13)

Directions: Complete the sentences with appropriate PRONOUNS and these PARTICLES:

away	*back*	*down*	*off*	*on*	*out*	*up*

1. When the children finished playing with *their toys*, they put _____**them away**_____.

2. If you don't want *your shirt* to get wrinkled, you'd better hang_____.

3. I wanted to see if *the shoes* were the right size, so I tried _____.

4. *The radio* was too loud, so I turned _____ a little.

5. I feel like talking to *Jim*. I think I'll call _____.

6. Rick poured some water on *the campfire* to put _____.

7. Whenever I borrow *money*, I make sure to pay _____ as soon as I can.

8. I can't hear *the TV*. Could you please turn _____? Thanks.

9. There's a phone message here from *Mary*. She sounds worried. You'd better call _____ as soon as possible.

10. If you leave *your computer* for a short while, you don't need to shut _____.

11. Because of crowd violence, *the championship match* was canceled. The authorities called _____.

12. No, Tommy, we're not going to buy *that candy bar*. Put _____ where you got it.

13. Tom invited *Linda* to go to a concert with him. In other words, he asked _____.

14. I'll lend you *my grammar book,* but be sure to give _____ to me before class tomorrow.

CHAPTER 11
The Passive

◇ PRACTICE 1—SELFSTUDY: Active vs. passive. (Chart 11-1)

Directions: Circle ACTIVE if the given sentence is active; circle PASSIVE if it is passive. <u>Underline</u> the VERB.

1.	(ACTIVE)	PASSIVE	Farmers <u>grow</u> corn.
2.	ACTIVE	(PASSIVE)	Corn <u>is grown</u> by farmers.
3.	ACTIVE	PASSIVE	Sara wrote the letter.
4.	ACTIVE	PASSIVE	The letter was written by Sara.
5.	ACTIVE	PASSIVE	The teacher explained the lesson.
6.	ACTIVE	PASSIVE	The lesson was explained by the teacher.
7.	ACTIVE	PASSIVE	Bridges are designed by engineers.
8.	ACTIVE	PASSIVE	Engineers design bridges.
9.	ACTIVE	PASSIVE	The mouse ate the cheese.
10.	ACTIVE	PASSIVE	The cheese was eaten by the mouse.

ACTIVE: → ATE →

PASSIVE: → WAS EATEN BY →

◇ PRACTICE 2—SELFSTUDY: Review of past participles. (Chart 2-3)

Directions: Write the PAST PARTICIPLES of the verbs. The list contains both regular and irregular verbs.

	SIMPLE FORM	SIMPLE PAST	PAST PARTICIPLE		SIMPLE FORM	SIMPLE PAST	PAST PARTICIPLE
1.	bring	brought	_**brought**_	14.	play	played	_____
2.	build	built	_____	15.	read	read*	_____
3.	buy	bought	_____	16.	save	saved	_____
4.	eat	ate	_____	17.	send	sent	_____
5.	plan	planned	_____	18.	speak	spoke	_____
6.	give	gave	_____	19.	spend	spent	_____
7.	grow	grew	_____	20.	take	took	_____
8.	hit	hit	_____	21.	teach	taught	_____
9.	hurt	hurt	_____	22.	go	went	_____
10.	leave	left	_____	23.	visit	visited	_____
11.	lose	lost	_____	24.	wear	wore	_____
12.	make	made	_____	25.	write	wrote	_____
13.	find	found	_____	26.	do	did	_____

◇ PRACTICE 3—SELFSTUDY: Passive form. (Charts 11-1, 11-2, and 11-6)

Directions: Use the given form of BE (WAS, IS, GOING TO BE, etc.) and complete the sentences with the PAST PARTICIPLES of any verbs in the list in Practice 2.

1. *was*   There's no more candy. All the candy _____**was eaten**_____ by the children.

2. *is*   Arabic _____ by the people of Syria and Iraq.

3. *are*   Books _____ by authors.

4. *was*   My friend _____ in an accident. He broke his nose.

5. *is going to be* Bombay, India, _____ by thousands of tourists this year.

6. *has been*   *War and Peace* is a famous book. It _____ by millions of people.

_____

*The simple past and past participle of *read* are pronounced "red," as the color red.

7. *will be*   The championship game _____ in Milan next

week.

8. *can be*   Everyone _____ to read. I'll teach you if you'd

like.

9. *are going to be*   Our pictures _____ by a professional

photographer at the wedding.

10. *have been*   Oranges _____ by farmers in Jordan since

ancient times.

11. *is*   Special fire-resistant clothing _____ by firefighters.

12. *will be*   A new bridge across the White River _____ by

the city government next year.

◇ PRACTICE 4—SELFSTUDY: Tense forms of the passive. (Chart 11-1 and 11-2)

Directions: Complete the sentences with the passive form of the given verbs.

PART I: Use the ***SIMPLE PRESENT*** with:

✔ collect	grow	understand
eat	pay	write

1. Taxes _____**are collected**_____ by the government.

2. Small fish _____ by big fish.

3. Rice _____ by farmers in Korea.

4. I _____ for my work by my boss.

5. Books _____ by authors.

6. The meaning of a smile _____ by everyone.

PART II: Use the ***SIMPLE PAST*** with:

build	collect	destroy	write

7. Yesterday the students' papers _____**were**_____ by the teacher at the end

of the test.

8. The Great Wall of China _____ by Chinese emperors over

2500 years ago.

9. The book *War and Peace* _____ by Leo Tolstoy, a famous

Russian novelist.

10. Several small buildings _____ by the recent earthquake in Los

Angeles.

PART III: Use the *PRESENT PERFECT* with:

     read   *speak*   *visit*   *wear*

11. The pyramids in Egypt _____*have*_____ by millions of tourists through the years.

12. Spanish _____ by people in Latin America for nearly 600 years.

13. Mark Twain's books _____ by millions of people through the years.

14. Perfume _____ by both men and women since ancient times.

PART IV: Use *WILL* with:

     discover   *visit*

15. New information about the universe _____*will*_____ by scientists in the twenty-first century.

16. Hawaii _____ by thousands of tourists this year.

PART V: Use *BE GOING TO* with:

     elect   *hurt*   *offer*   *save*

17. Your friend _____*is going*_____ by your unkind remark when she hears about it.

18. New computer courses _____ by the university next year.

19. Tigers _____ from extinction by people who care.

20. A new leader _____ by the people in my country next month.

◇ PRACTICE 5—SELFSTUDY: Passive to active. (Charts 6-2, 11-1 and 11-2)

    Directions: Change the passive sentences to ACTIVE. Keep the same verb tense.

1. Taxes are collected by the government. → *The government collects taxes.*

2. Small fish are eaten by big fish.

3. The meaning of a smile is understood by everyone.

4. *War and Peace* was written by Leo Tolstoy.

5. The pyramids in Egypt have been visited by millions of tourists.

6. New information about the universe will be discovered by scientists in the twenty-first century.

◇ PRACTICE 6—SELFSTUDY: Passive to active. (Charts 6-2, 11-1 and 11-2)

Directions: Change the passive sentences to ACTIVE. Keep the same tense. Some of the sentences are questions.

1. The letter was signed by Mr. Rice. → *Mr. Rice signed the letter.*

2. Was the letter signed by Mr. Foster? → *Did Mr. Foster sign the letter?*

3. The fax was sent by Ms. Owens.

4. Was the other fax sent by Mr. Chu?

5. Will Adam be met at the airport by Mr. Berg?

6. Adam will be met at the airport by Mrs. Berg.

7. Have you been invited to the reception by Mrs. Jordan?

8. I have been invited to the reception by Mr. Lee.

9. Is the homework going to be collected by the teacher?

10. The homework is going to be collected by the teacher.

◇ PRACTICE 7—GUIDED STUDY: Passive to active. (Charts 6-2, 11-1 and 11-2)

Directions: Change the passive sentences to active. Keep the same tense. Some of the sentences are questions.

1. Were you taught to read by your parents?

   → *Did your parents teach you to read?*

2. I was taught to read by my parents.

   → *My parents taught me to read.*

3. Was the riot stopped by the police?

4. Love and understanding are needed by all children.

5. The ball was kicked by the captain of the soccer team.

6. Was the chalkboard washed by a student?

7. My suitcase was inspected by a customs officer.

8. Are we going to be met at the train station by your cousin?

9. The plans for the new hospital have already been drawn by the architect.

10. The bear was chased up a tree by a dog.

◇ PRACTICE 8—SELFSTUDY: Transitive vs. intransitive. (Chart 11-3)

Directions: Circle TRANSITIVE if the verb takes an object; circle INTRANSITIVE if it does not. <u>Underline</u> the OBJECT OF THE VERB.

1. (TRANSITIVE) INTRANSITIVE   Alex wrote <u>a letter</u>.

2. TRANSITIVE (INTRANSITIVE)   Alex waited for Amy. *(There is no object of the verb.)*

3. TRANSITIVE INTRANSITIVE   Rita lives in Mexico.

4.	TRANSITIVE	INTRANSITIVE	Sam walked to his office.
5.	TRANSITIVE	INTRANSITIVE	Kate caught the ball.
6.	TRANSITIVE	INTRANSITIVE	My plane arrived at six-thirty.
7.	TRANSITIVE	INTRANSITIVE	Emily is crying.
8.	TRANSITIVE	INTRANSITIVE	A falling tree hit my car.
9.	TRANSITIVE	INTRANSITIVE	I returned the book to the library yesterday.
10.	TRANSITIVE	INTRANSITIVE	A bolt of lightning appeared in the sky last night.

◇ PRACTICE 9—SELFSTUDY: Active and passive. (Charts 11-1 → 11-3)

Directions: <u>Underline</u> the OBJECT OF THE VERB if the given sentence has one. Then change the sentence to the passive. Some sentences cannot be changed to the passive.

ACTIVE	PASSIVE
1. A noise awakened <u>me</u>.	**I *was awakened by a noise.***
2. It rained hard yesterday.	(*no change*)
3. Alice discovered the mistake.	_____
4. We stayed at a hotel last night.	_____
5. Dinosaurs existed millions of years ago.	_____
6. I usually agree with my sister.	_____
7. Many people die during a war.	_____
8. In the fairy tale, a princess kissed a frog.	_____
9. I slept only four hours last night.	_____
10. Anita fixed the chair.	_____
11. Did Susan agree with Prof. Hill?	_____
12. Did the Koreans invent gunpowder?	_____
13. The /th/ sound doesn't occur in my native language.	_____
14. Research scientists will discover a cure for AIDS* someday.	_____
15. A cloud of migrating butterflies appeared out of nowhere.	_____

_____

*AIDS = a disease (**A**uto **I**mmune **D**eficiency **S**yndrome).

◇ PRACTICE 10—SELFSTUDY: The *by*-phrase. (Chart 11-4)

Directions: If the sentence contains a BY-phrase, underline it. Then answer the question. If you don't know the exact person or people who performed the action, write UNKNOWN. (NOTE: Most of the sentences are passive, but some are active.)

1. The mail is usually delivered to Bob's apartment around eleven o'clock.
   Who delivers the mail?   **unknown**

2. The wastebasket was emptied by Fred.
   Who emptied the wastebasket?   **Fred**

3. Paul carried the suitcases into the airport for his elderly father.
   Who carried the suitcases?

4. The Eiffel Tower was designed by Alexandre Eiffel.
   Who designed the Eiffel Tower?

5. The Eiffel Tower was erected in 1889.
   Who erected the Eiffel Tower?

6. Nicole visited the Eiffel Tower when she was in France last year.
   Who visited the Eiffel Tower?

7. Our classroom building was built in the 1950s.
   Who built the classroom building?

8. Our exam papers will be corrected by Ms. Brown.
   Who will correct the exam papers?

9. Coffee is grown in Brazil.
   Who grows coffee in Brazil?

10. Sara accepted Mike's invitation to the international street fair next Saturday.
    Who accepted the invitation?

11. Eric Wong's new book will be translated into many languages.
    Who will translate Eric Wong's new book?

12. Rebecca's bicycle was stolen yesterday from in front of the library.
    Who stole Rebecca's bicycle?

◇ PRACTICE 11—GUIDED STUDY: The *by*-phrase. (Chart 11-4)

Directions: Underline the passive verbs. Answer the questions. If you don't know the exact person or people who performed the action, write UNKNOWN.

1. Soft duck feathers are used to make pillows.
   Who uses duck feathers to make pillows?   **unknown**

2. The mail was opened by Shelley.
   Who opened the mail?   **Shelley**

3. All the tickets for the school play tonight have been sold.
   Who sold the tickets to the school play?

4. My flight was canceled because of the heavy fog.
   Who canceled the flight?

5. Aunt Mary's favorite glass bowl was accidentally broken by her nephew David.
   Who broke the glass bowl?

6. Malawi is a country in southeastern Africa. A new highway is going to be built in Malawi next year.
   Who is going to build the new highway?

7. The invention of the printing press changed the world because it allowed many people instead of few to have copies of books. It was invented by Johannes Gutenberg around 1440. Before that, people wrote books by hand. Writing books by hand was a slow process.
Who invented the printing press?

8. One of the most significant inventions in the history of civilization is the wheel. It was invented around five thousand years ago. It allowed people to pull things in carts instead of carrying everything on their backs or in their arms.
Who invented the wheel?

9. Yesterday there was almost a tragedy at the swimming pool. A young boy who didn't know how to swim jumped in the deep end. He panicked★ when he couldn't swim to the side of the pool. He was saved from drowning by a lifeguard at the pool. It's lucky that she was alert.
Who saved the boy?

10. The name *Thailand* means "land of the free." The Thai people have never been ruled by a foreign power. Thailand is a constitutional monarchy. The prime minister is nominated by the National Assembly and then is appointed by the monarch. Senators are chosen by the prime minister and representatives are elected by the people.
Who nominates the prime minister?
Who appoints the prime minister?
Who chooses the senators?
Who elects the representatives?
What countries have ruled Thailand?

★*To panic* is a verb that means "to become suddenly and greatly frightened." Notice that a "k" is added before the *-ed* ending.

◇ PRACTICE 12—SELFSTUDY: Active vs. passive. (Charts 11-1 → 11-4)

Directions: Complete the sentences with the correct forms of the verbs in parentheses.

1. Almost everyone (enjoy) _____ ***enjoys*** _____ visiting a zoo. Today zoos are common.

2. The first zoo (establish) _____ around 3500 years ago by an Egyptian queen for her personal enjoyment. Five hundred years later, a Chinese emperor (establish) _____ a huge zoo to show his power and wealth. Later zoos (establish) _____ for the purpose of studying animals.

3. Some of the early European zoos were dark holes or dirty cages. People (disgust) _____ by the bad conditions and the mistreatment of the animals. In the nineteenth century, these early zoos (replace) _____ by scientific institutions where animals (study) _____ and (keep) _____ in good condition. These research centers (become) _____ the first modern zoos.

4. As early as the 1940s, scientists (understand) _____ that many kinds of wild animals faced extinction. Since that time, zoos (become) _____ a place to save many endangered species such as the rhinoceros. In the 1980s, the number of rhinos in the world (reduce) _____ from 10,000 to 400. Some wildlife biologists fear that the species (become) _____ extinct in the wild in the near future. Some scientists (believe) _____ that half of the animal species in zoos will be in danger of extinction by the middle of the twenty-first century.

5. Because zoos want to treat animals humanely and encourage breeding, animals (put, now) _____ in large, natural settings instead of small cages. They (watch) _____ carefully for any signs of disease and (feed) _____ a balanced diet. Most zoos (have) _____ a hospital for animals and specially trained veterinarians.

6. Today food (prepare) _____ in the zoo kitchen. The food program (design) _____ to satisfy the animals' particular needs. For example, some snakes (feed) _____ only once a week, and some birds (feed) _____ several times a day.

7. Today zoo animals (treat) _____ well, and zoo breeding programs are important in the attempt to save many species of wildlife.

◇ PRACTICE 13—SELFSTUDY: Progressive tenses in passive. (Chart 11-5)

Directions: <u>Underline</u> the PROGRESSIVE VERB. Then complete the sentence with the correct PASSIVE form.

1. Some people <u>are considering</u> a new plan.

→ A new plan _____ ***is being considered*** _____.

2. The grandparents are watching the children.

→ The children _____ by their grandparents.

3. Some painters are painting Mr. Rivera's apartment this week.

→ Mr. Rivera's apartment _____ this week.

4. Many of the older people in the neighborhood were growing vegetables.

→ Vegetables _____ by many of the older people in the

neighborhood.

5. Eric's cousins are meeting him at the airport this afternoon.

→ Eric _____ by his cousins at the airport this afternoon.

6. I watched while the movers were moving the furniture from my apartment to a truck.

→ I watched while the furniture _____ from my apartment

to a truck.

◇ PRACTICE 14—GUIDED STUDY: Progressive tenses in passive. (Chart 11-5)

Directions: Complete the sentences with the correct PASSIVE form.

1. Mr. Rice is teaching our class today.

→ Our class _____ ***is being taught*** _____ by Mr. Rice today.

2. Scientists are still discovering new species of plants and animals.

→ New species of plants and animals _____.

3. Everyone looked at the flag while they were singing the national anthem.

→ Everyone looked at the flag while the national anthem _____.

4. Dogs usually wag their tails while people are petting them.

→ Dogs usually wag their tails while they _____.

5. According to one scientific estimate, we are losing 20,000 species of plants and animals each

year due to the destruction of rain forests.

→ According to one scientific estimate, 20,000 species of plants and animals

_____ each year due to the destruction of rain forests.

◇ PRACTICE 15—GUIDED STUDY: Active vs. passive. (Charts 11-1 → 11-7)

Directions: Circle ACTIVE if the sentence is active; circle PASSIVE if it is passive. <u>Underline</u> the verb.

1. (ACTIVE) PASSIVE   People <u>have used</u> sundials since ancient times.

2. ACTIVE (PASSIVE)   Sundials <u>have been used</u> for almost three thousand years.

3. ACTIVE PASSIVE   Sundials, clocks, and watches are used to tell time.

4. ACTIVE PASSIVE   Some watches show the date as well as the time.

5. ACTIVE PASSIVE   On digital watches, the time is shown by lighted numbers.

6. ACTIVE PASSIVE   The first watches were made in Europe six hundred years ago.

7. ACTIVE PASSIVE   The earliest watches were worn around a person's neck.

8. ACTIVE PASSIVE   Pocket watches became popular in the 1600s.

9. ACTIVE PASSIVE   Today most people wear wristwatches.

10. ACTIVE PASSIVE   Close to seventy million watches are sold in the United States each year.

11. ACTIVE PASSIVE   How many watches are made and sold throughout the world in one year?

12. ACTIVE PASSIVE   Somewhere in the world, a watch is being sold at this very moment.

13. ACTIVE PASSIVE   Many different styles of watches can be bought today.

14. ACTIVE PASSIVE   Do you own a watch?

15. ACTIVE PASSIVE   Where was it made?

16. ACTIVE PASSIVE   Some watches can be worn underwater.

DO YOU HAVE THE TIME?

◇ PRACTICE 16—SELFSTUDY: Passive modals. (Chart 11-6)

Directions: Complete the sentences by changing the active modals to PASSIVE MODALS.

1. Someone must send this letter immediately.

   → This letter _____ ***must be sent*** _____ immediately.

2. You can find flowers in almost every part of the world.

   → Flowers _____ in almost every part of the world.

3. Someone ought to wash these dirty dishes soon.

   → These dirty dishes _____ soon.

4. People may cook carrots or eat them raw.

   → Carrots _____ or _____ raw.

5. Our air conditioner doesn't work. Someone has to fix it before the hot weather comes.

   → Our air conditioner _____ before the hot weather comes.

6. If the river floods, water might destroy the village.

   → The village _____ if the river floods.

7. Someone may call off the picnic if it rains.

   → The picnic _____ if it rains.

8. You must keep medicine out of the reach of children.

   → Medicine _____ out of the reach of children.

9. You shouldn't pronounce the "b" in "lamb."

   → The "b" in "lamb" _____.

10. People should remove coffee stains on cotton immediately with cold water.

    → Coffee stains on cotton _____ immediately with cold water.

◇ PRACTICE 17—GUIDED STUDY: Passive modals. (Chart 11-6)

Directions: Complete the sentences by using the words in the list with the MODALS in parentheses. All of the completions are PASSIVE.

build	know	teach
divide	✔ put off	tear down
kill	sell	write

1. Don't postpone things you need to do. Important work _____ ***shouldn't be put off*** _____ until the last minute. *(should not)*

2. Your application letter _____ in ink, not pencil. *(must)*

3. Dogs _____ to do tricks. *(can)*

4. Mrs. Papadopolous didn't want her son to go to war because he _____

_____. *(could)*

5. My son's class is too big. It _____ into two classes. *(ought to)*

6. A: Hey, Tony. These bananas are getting too ripe. They _____

today. Reduce the price. *(must)*

B: Right away, Mr. Rice.

7. It takes time to correct an examination that is taken by ten thousand students nationwide. The

test results _____ for at least four weeks. *(will not)*

8. The big bank building on Main Street was severely damaged in the earthquake. The structure

is no longer strong or safe. The building _____. Then

a new bank _____ in the same place. *(has to, can)*

◇ PRACTICE 18—SELFSTUDY: Active vs. passive. (Charts 11-1 → 11-7)

Directions: Complete the sentences with the verbs in parentheses; use ACTIVE or PASSIVE.

1. Flowers *(love)* _____ **are loved** _____ throughout the world. Their beauty

(bring) _____ **brings** _____ joy to people's lives. Flowers *(use, often)*

_____ to decorate homes or tables in restaurants. Public

gardens *(can find)* _____ in almost every country in the world.

2. Around 250,000 different kinds of flowers *(exist)* _____ in the

world. The majority of these species *(can find)* _____ only in

the tropics. Nontropical areas *(have)* _____ many fewer kinds

of flowering plants than tropical regions.

3. Flowers may spread from their native region to other similar regions. Sometimes seeds *(carry)*

_____ by birds or animals. The wind also *(carry)*

_____ some seeds. In many cases throughout history,

flowering plants *(introduce)* _____ into new areas by humans.

4. Flowers *(appreciate)* _____ mostly for their beauty, but they

can also be a source of food. For example, honey *(make)* _____

from the nectar which *(gather)* _____ from flowers by bees.

And some flower buds *(eat)* _____ as food; for example,

broccoli and cauliflower are actually flower buds.

5. Some very expensive perfumes *(make)* _____ from the petals

   of flowers. Most perfumes today, however, *(come, not)* _____

   from natural fragrances. Instead, they are synthethic; they *(make)* _____

   from chemicals in a laboratory.

6. Some kinds of flowers *(may plant)* _____ in pots and *(grow)*

   _____ indoors. Most flowers, however, *(survive)*

   _____ best outdoors in their usual environment.

◇ PRACTICE 19—GUIDED STUDY: Active vs. passive. (Charts 11-1 → 11-7)

> Directions: All of the sentences in the following passage are active. Some of the sentences should
> be passive because it is unknown or unimportant to know exactly who performs certain actions.
> Change sentences to the PASSIVE AS APPROPRIATE. Discuss your reasons for making changes and
> for not making changes.

(1) Cheese has been a principal food throughout much of the world for thousands of years.

The first cheese was probably made
(2) ~~Someone probably made the first cheese~~ in Asia around four thousand years ago.

(3) Today people eat it in almost all the countries of the world.   (4) People can eat it alone, or

they may eat it with bread.   (5) People can melt it and add it to noodles or vegetables.

(6) People can use it as part of a main course or as a snack.   (7) Throughout most of the

world, cheese adds enjoyment and nutrition to many people's daily diets.

(8) Cheese is a milk product.   (9) Cheesemakers make most cheese from cow's milk, but

they can make it from the milk of goats, camels, yaks and other animals, including zebras.

(10) Some kinds of cheese, such as cheddar, are common in many parts in the world, but you

can find other kinds only in small geographical areas.

(11) Cheesemakers produce cheese in factories.   (12) They have to treat the milk in

special ways.   (13) They must heat it several times during the process.   (14) At the end, they

add salt and they pack it into molds.   (15) They age most cheese for weeks or months before

they package and sell it.   (16) They usually sell cheese to stores in large round pieces that

they seal in wax.

(17) You can see these big rounds of cheese in food stores like delicatessens. (18) I like cheese and buy it often. (19) I don't know all the names of different kinds of cheese. (20) Often I can't pronounce the foreign name of the cheese I want. (21) When I go to the delicatessen near my apartment, I simply point to a kind of cheese that looks good to me. (22) I hold my thumb and forefinger wide apart if I want a lot of cheese or close together if I want just a little. (23) Frank and Anita, who work behind the cheese counter at the deli, always seem to give me just the right amount. (24) I'm glad cheese is nutritious because it's one of my favorite kinds of food.

◇ PRACTICE 20—SELFSTUDY: Stative passive. (Chart 11-8)

Directions: Complete the sentences with the appropriate form, ACTIVE or PASSIVE, of the verbs in parentheses. Include PREPOSITIONS as necessary. Use the SIMPLE PRESENT.

1. Loud noises _____**scare**_____ small children. *(scare)*

2. Most children _____**are scared of**_____ loud noises. *(scare)*

3. New ideas _____ me. *(interest)*

4. Jane _____ ecology. *(interest)*

5. My bad grades _____ my parents. *(disappoint)*

6. My parents _____ me because of my low grades. *(disappoint)*

7. My boss _____ my work. *(please)*

8. My work _____ my boss. *(please)*

9. My progress in English _____ me. *(satisfy)*

10. I _____ my progress in English. *(satisfy)*

◇ PRACTICE 21—SELFSTUDY: Participial adjectives. (Chart 11-9)

Directions: Complete the sentences with the appropriate **-ED** or **-ING** form of the words in parentheses.

Ben is reading a book. He really likes it. He can't put it down. He has to keep reading.

1. The book is really _____**interesting**_____. *(interest)*

2. Ben is really _____. *(interest)*

3. The story is _____. *(excite)*

4. Ben is _____ about the story. *(excite)*

5. Ben is _____ by the characters in the book. *(fascinate)*

6. The people in the story are _____. *(fascinate)*

7. Ben doesn't like to read books when he is _____ and
_____. *(bore, confuse)*

8. Ben didn't finish that last book he started because it was _____ and
_____. *(bore, confuse)*

9. What is the most _____ book you've read lately? *(interest)*

10. I just finished a _____ mystery story that had a very
_____ ending. *(fascinate, surprise)*

Directions: Complete the sentences with the appropriate -ED or -ING form of the words in parentheses.

Julie was walking along the edge of the fountain outside her office building. She was with her co-worker and friend Paul. Suddenly she lost her balance and accidentally fell in.

1. Julie was really _____. *(embarrass)*

2. Falling into the fountain was really _____. *(embarrass)*

3. Her friend Paul was _____. *(shock)*

4. It was a _____ sight. *(shock)*

5. The people around the office building were very _____ when they saw Julie in the fountain. *(surprise)*

6. It was a _____ sight. *(surprise)*

7. The next day Julie was _____ because she thought she had made a fool of herself. *(depress)*

8. When she fell into the fountain, some people laughed at her. It was a _____ experience. *(depress)*

9. Her friend Paul told her not to lose her sense of humor. He told her it was just another _____ experience in life. *(interest)*

10. He said that people would be _____ in hearing about how she fell into a fountain. *(interest)*

◇ PRACTICE 23—GUIDED STUDY: Participial adjectives. (Chart 11-9)

Directions: Complete the sentences with your own words.

Example: I'm bored . . . .
→ *I am bored by people who talk about themselves all the time.*

Example: . . . is/are boring.
→ *Self-centered people are boring.*

1. I am interested in . . . .
2. . . . is/are interesting to me.
3. I am fascinated by . . . .
4. . . . is/are fascinating to me.
5. . . . is/are exciting.
6. . . . is/are confusing.
7. I was excited when . . . .
8. I was confused when . . . .
9. I was surprised when . . . .
10. I'll be surprised if . . . .

◇ PRACTICE 24—SELFSTUDY: *Get* + adjective and past participle. (Chart 11-10)

Directions: Complete the sentences with appropriate forms of **GET** and the words in the given list.

busy	dress	invite	tired
dark	dry	marry	well
dizzy	hungry	✔sunburn	wet

1. When I stayed out in the sun too long yesterday, I _____ **got sunburned** _____ .

2. If you're sick, stay home and take care of yourself. You won't _____ if you don't take care of yourself.

3. Jane and Greg are engaged. They are going to _____ a year from now.

4. Sarah doesn't eat breakfast, so she always _____ by ten or ten-thirty.

5. In the winter, the sun sets early. It _____ outside by six or even earlier.

6. Yes, I have an invitation to Joan and Paul's wedding. Don't worry. You'll _____

   _____ to the wedding, too.

7. Put these socks back in the dryer. They didn't _____ the first time.

8. Let's stop working for a while. I'm _____ . I need to rest.

9. Sam is wearing one brown sock and one blue sock today. He _____ in a hurry this morning and didn't pay attention to the color of his socks.

10. This work has to be done before we leave. We'd better _____ and stop wasting time.

11. Some people are afraid of heights. They _____ and have trouble keeping their balance.

12. Sally _____ when she stood near the pool of dolphins. They splashed her more than once.

◇ PRACTICE 25—GUIDED STUDY: *Get* + adjective and past participle. (Chart 11-10)

Directions: Complete the sentences with appropriate forms of **GET** and the words in the given list.

cold	*excite*	*lose*	*steal*
crowd	*involve*	*rich*	*thirsty*
dirty	*kill*	*sleepy*	✔ *worry*

1. Sue has to vacate her apartment next week, and she hasn't found a new place to live. She's

   _____**getting worried**_____.

2. Sitara always _____ after she eats salty food.

3. Toshiro was in a terrible car wreck and almost _____. He's lucky to be alive.

4. The temperature is dropping. Brrr! I'm _____. Can I borrow your sweater?

5. We were in a strange city without a map. It was easy for us to _____. We had to ask a shopkeeper how to get back to our hotel.

6. Did you _____ when your team won the game? Did you clap and yell when they won?

7. Good restaurants _____ around dinner time. It's hard to find a seat because there are so many people.

8. When little Annie _____, her father gave her a bottle and put her to bed.

9. It's hard to work in a garage and stay clean. Paul's clothes always _____ from all the grease and oil.

10. Don't waste your money gambling. You won't ever _____ that way.

11. Tarik was afraid his important papers or his jewelry might _____, so he had a wall safe installed in his home.

12. I left when Ellen and Joe began to argue. I never _____ in other people's quarrels.

◇ PRACTICE 26—SELFSTUDY: *Used to* vs. *be accustomed to.* (Charts 2-9 and 11-11)

Directions: Choose the correct completions. **More than one** completion may be correct.

1. Frank has lived alone for twenty years. He __**B, C**__ alone.
   A. used to live B. is used to living C. is accustomed to living

2. I ____**A**____ with my family, but now I live alone.
   A. used to live B. am used to living C. am accustomed to living

3. Rita rides her bike to work every day. She _____ her bike to work.
   A. used to ride B. is used to riding C. is accustomed to riding

4. Tom rode his bike to work for many years, but now he takes the bus. Tom _____ his bike to work.
   A. used to ride B. is used to riding C. is accustomed to riding

5. Carl showers every day. He _____ a shower every day.
   A. used to take B. is used to taking C. is accustomed to taking

6. Carl _____ a bath only once a week, but now he showers every day.
   A. used to take B. is used to taking C. is accustomed to taking

◇ PRACTICE 27—SELFSTUDY: *Used to* vs. *be used to.* (Charts 2-9 and 11-11)

Directions: Complete the sentences with USED TO or BE USED TO/BE ACCUSTOMED TO and the correct form of the verb in parentheses.

1. Nick stays up later now than he did when he was in high school. He *(go)*

   _____**used to go**_____ to bed at ten, but now he rarely gets to bed before midnight.

2. I got used to going to bed late when I was in college, but now I have a job and I need my sleep.

   These days I *(go)* ____**am used to going/am accustomed to going**____ to bed

   around ten-thirty.

3. I am a vegetarian. I *(eat)* _____ meat, but now I eat only meatless

   meals.

4. Mrs. Wu has had a vegetable garden all her life. She *(grow)* _____

   her own vegetables.

5. Oscar has lived in Brazil for ten years. He *(eat)* _____ Brazilian food.

   He doesn't like any other kind.

6. Georgio moved to Germany to open his own restaurant. He *(have)* _____

   a small bakery in Italy.

7. I have taken the bus to work every day for the past five years. I *(take)* _____

   the bus.

8. Juanita travels by plane on company business. She *(go)* _____ by train,

   but now the distances she needs to travel are too great.

◇ PRACTICE 28—GUIDED STUDY: *Be used/accustomed to* and *get used/accustomed to.* (Chart 11-11)

Directions: Discuss or write about the following topics.

1. James graduated from high school last month. Three days after graduation, he got married. The next week he got a job at a paint store. Within two weeks, his life changed a lot. What did he have to get used to?

2. Jane is going to leave her parents' house next week. She is going to move in with two of her cousins who work in the city. Jane will be away from her home for the first time in her life. What is she going to have to get used to?

3. Think of a time you traveled in or lived in a foreign country. What weren't you used to? What did you get used to? What didn't you ever get used to?

4. Think of the first day of a job you have had. What weren't you used to? What did you get used to?

◇ PRACTICE 29—SELFSTUDY: *Be supposed to.* (Chart 11-12)

Directions: Find the mistakes and correct them.

1. INCORRECT: I'm supposed ^**to** call my parents tonight.

2. INCORRECT: We're not suppose to tell anyone about the surprise.

3. INCORRECT: You don't supposed to talk to Alan about the surprise.

4. INCORRECT: My friend was supposing to call me last night, but he didn't.

5. INCORRECT: Children supposed to respect their parents.

6. INCORRECT: Didn't you supposed be at the meeting last night?

◇ PRACTICE 30—SELFSTUDY: *Be supposed to.* (Chart 11-12)

Directions: Make sentences with **BE SUPPOSED TO** by combining the subjects in Column A with the ideas in Column B. Use the SIMPLE PRESENT.

Example: Doctors are supposed to care about their patients.

COLUMN A

1. Doctors
2. Visitors at a zoo
3. Employees
4. Air passengers
5. Theatergoers
6. Soldiers on sentry duty
7. Children
8. Heads of state
9. A dog
10. People who live in apartments

COLUMN B

A. listen to their parents
B. buckle their seatbelts before takeoff
C. not . . . feed the animals
D. not . . . talk during a performance
E. be on time for work
F. obey its trainer
G. pay their rent on time
✔H. care about their patients
I. not . . . fall asleep
J. be diplomatic

◇ PRACTICE 31—GUIDED STUDY: *Be supposed to.* (Chart 11-12)

Directions: Think of things the following people are or were supposed to do. Use BE SUPPOSED TO.

Example: a good friend of yours

→ *My friend Ji Ming is supposed to help me paint my apartment this weekend.*
Benito was supposed to go to dinner with me last Wednesday, but he forgot.
Nadia is supposed to call me tonight.

1. a good friend of yours
2. your roommate or spouse*
3. children
4. a student in your English class
5. your English teacher
6. the leader of your country
7. one or both of your parents
8. one of your siblings or cousins
9. yourself
10. (. . .)

◇ PRACTICE 32—GUIDED STUDY: Verb form review. (Chapters 1 → 11)

Directions: Complete the sentences by writing the correct form of the verb in parentheses.

What is your most *(1. embarrass)* _____ experience? Let me tell you what

happened to my uncle when he *(2. go)* _____ to Norway for a business

meeting last year.

First, I must tell you about my Uncle Ernesto. He *(3. be)* _____ a

businessman from Buenos Aires, Argentina. He *(4. manufacture)* _____ a

new kind of computer compass for ships. Computer compasses *(5. manufacture)*

_____ by many companies in the world, so my uncle *(6. have)*

_____ a lot of competition for his product. In order to sell his product, he

(7. need) _____ *(8. meet)* _____ with companies that

might want to buy it. He *(9. travel)* _____ frequently to other countries.

Last year, he *(10. go)* _____ to Norway *(11. meet)* _____

with a shipping company. It was his first trip to Europe. My Uncle Ernesto *(12. speak)*

_____ Spanish, of course, and also *(13. know)* _____

_____

*If you have neither a roommate nor a spouse, invent one or simply skip to the next item.

a little English, but he *(14. know, not)* _____ any Norwegian. While he

(15. stay) _____ in Norway, he *(16. have)* _____ a

problem.

Uncle Ernesto *(17. stay)* _____ at a large, modern hotel in Oslo. One

morning, while he *(18. get)* _____ ready to take a shower, he *(19. hear)*

_____ a knock at the door. He *(20. walk)* _____ to the

door, *(21. open)* _____ it, and *(22. find)* _____ no one.

He *(23. take)* _____ a step out of his room and *(24. look)* _____

down the hall. He *(25. see)* _____ no one. So he *(26. turn)*

_____ *(27. go)* _____ back into his room, but the door

(28. close) _____! It *(29. lock)* _____, and he *(30. have,*

not) _____ his key. This was a very big problem for my uncle because he

(31. dress, not) _____ properly. In fact, he *(32. wear)* _____

nothing but a towel. Poor Uncle Ernesto! "What *(33. do, I)* _____?" he

asked himself.

Instead of *(34. stand)* _____ in the hallway with only a towel, he

(35. decide) _____ *(36. get)* _____ help. So he

(37. start) _____ *(38. walk)* _____ down the hall toward

the elevator. He was too *(39. embarrass)* _____ *(40. knock)* _____

on someone else's door *(41. ask)* _____ for help.

When he *(42. reach)* _____ the elevator, he *(43. push)* _____

the down button and *(44. wait)* _____. When it *(45. come)* _____,

Uncle Ernesto *(46. take)* _____ a deep breath and *(47. get)* _____

into the elevator. The other people in the elevator *(48. surprise)* _____ when

they *(49. see)* _____ a man who *(50. wrap)* _____ in a towel.

Uncle Ernesto *(51. think)* _____ about *(52. try)* _____

(53. explain) _____ his problem, but he *(54. know, not)*

_____ any Norwegian. He said, in English, "Door. Locked. No key." A

businessman in the elevator *(55. nod)* _____, but he *(56. smile, not)*

_____. Another man *(57. look)* _____ at Uncle

Ernesto and *(58. smile)* _____ broadly.

After an eternity, the elevator *(59. reach)* _____ the ground floor. Uncle Ernesto *(60. walk)* _____ straight to the front desk and *(61. look)* _____ at the hotel manager helplessly. The hotel manager *(62. have to understand, not)* _____ any language *(63. figure)* _____ out the problem. My uncle *(64. have to say, not)* _____ _____ a word. The manager *(65. grab)* _____ a key, *(66. take)* _____ my uncle by the elbow, and *(67. lead)* _____ _____ him to the nearest elevator.

My uncle *(68. embarrass, still)* _____ about this incident. But he always *(69. laugh)* _____ a lot when he *(70. tell)* _____ the story.

CHAPTER *12*
Adjective Clauses

◇ PRACTICE 1—SELFSTUDY: Using *who* in adjective clauses. (Charts 12-1 → 12-2)

Directions: Find and <u>underline</u> the ADJECTIVE CLAUSE in the long sentence. Then complete the change of the long sentence into two short sentences.*

1. *Long sentence:*   I thanked the man <u>who helped me move the refrigerator.</u>

   Short sentence 1: _____**I thanked**_____ the man.

   Short sentence 2: _____**He helped**_____ me move the refrigerator.

2. *Long sentence:*   A woman who was wearing a gray suit asked me for directions.

   Short sentence 1: _____ me for directions.

   Short sentence 2: _____ a gray suit.

3. *Long sentence:*   I saw a man who was wearing a blue coat.

   Short sentence 1: _____ a man.

   Short sentence 2: _____ a blue coat.

4. *Long sentence:*   The woman who aided the rebels put her life in danger.

   Short sentence 1: _____ her life in danger.

   Short sentence 2: _____ the rebels.

---

*In grammar terminology, the "long sentence" is called **a complex sentence** and the "short sentence" is called **a simple sentence**:

- A complex sentence has an independent clause and a dependent clause. For example:
  I thanked the man who helped me. = a complex sentence consisting of one independent clause (*I thanked the man*) and one dependent clause (*who helped me*).
- A simple sentence has only an independent clause. For example:
  I thanked the man. = a simple sentence consisting of one independent clause.
  He helped me. = a simple sentence consisting of one independent clause.

5. *Long sentence:*   I know some people who live on a boat.

   Short sentence 1: _____ some people.

   Short sentence 2: _____ on a boat.

◇ PRACTICE 2—SELFSTUDY: Using *who* in adjective clauses. (Chart 12-2)

   Directions: Combine the two short sentences into one long sentence using "sentence 2" as an ADJECTIVE CLAUSE. Use **WHO**. <u>Underline</u> the adjective clause.

1. *Short sentence 1:*   The woman was polite.
   Short sentence 2:   She answered the phone.

   Long sentence: **The woman <u>who answered the phone</u> was polite.**

2. *Short sentence 1:*   The man has a good voice.
   Short sentence 2:   He sang at the concert.

   Long sentence:

3. *Short sentence 1:*   We enjoyed the actors.
   Short sentence 2:   They played the leading roles.

   Long sentence:

4. *Short sentence 1:*   The girl is hurt.
   Short sentence 2:   She fell down the stairs.

   Long sentence:

◇ PRACTICE 3—SELFSTUDY: Using *who* in adjective clauses. (Chart 12-2)

Directions: Insert **WHO** where it is necessary.

1. The man ᴬ answered the phone was polite.
   who

2. I liked the people sat next to us at the soccer game.

3. People paint houses for a living are called house painters.

4. I'm uncomfortable around married couples argue all the time.

5. While I was waiting at the bus stop, I stood next to an elderly gentleman started a conversation

   with me about my educational plans.

◇ PRACTICE 4—SELFSTUDY: Using *who* and *whom* in adjective clauses. (Chart 12-2)

Directions: Find and <u>underline</u> the ADJECTIVE CLAUSE. Identify the SUBJECT and VERB of the
adjective clause. Then complete the change from one long sentence to two short sentences, and
identify the SUBJECT and VERB of the second short sentence.

1. *Long sentence:*   The people <u>who live next to me</u> are nice.
                                                                       S **V**
   Short sentence 1: The people are nice.
                                       S   **V**
   Short sentence 2: **They live next to me.**

2. *Long sentence:*   The people <u>whom Kate visited yesterday</u> were French.
                                                                 S   **V**
   Short sentence 1: The people were French.
                                       S   **V**
   Short sentence 2: **Kate visited them yesterday.**

3. *Long sentence:*   The people whom I saw at the park were having a picnic.
   Short sentence 1: The people were having a picnic.

   Short sentence 2:

4. *Long sentence:*   The students who go to this school are friendly.
   Short sentence 1: The students are friendly.

   Short sentence 2:

5. *Long sentence:*   The woman whom you met last week lives in Mexico.
   Short sentence 1: The woman lives in Mexico.

   Short sentence 2:

◇ PRACTICE 5—SELFSTUDY: Using *who* and *whom* in adjective clauses. (Chart 12-2)

Directions: Change the two short sentences into one long sentence with an ADJECTIVE CLAUSE. Use **WHO** or **WHOM**. <u>Underline</u> the adjective clause.

1. *Short sentence 1:* The woman was polite.
   Short sentence 2: Jack met her.

   Long sentence: **The woman <u>whom Jack met</u> was polite.**

2. *Short sentence 1:* I like the woman.
   Short sentence 2: She manages my uncle's store.

   Long sentence: **I like the woman <u>who manages my uncle's store</u>.**

3. *Short sentence 1:* The singer was wonderful.
   Short sentence 2: We heard him at the concert.

   Long sentence:

4. *Short sentence 1:* The people brought a small gift.
   Short sentence 2: They came to dinner.

   Long sentence:

5. *Short sentence 1:* What is the name of the woman?
   Short sentence 2: Tom invited her to the dance.

   Long sentence:

◇ PRACTICE 6—SELFSTUDY: Using *who* and *who(m)* in adjective clauses. (Chart 12-2)

Directions: Complete the sentences with **WHO** or **WHO(M)**.★

1. I know a man _____*who*_____ works at the post office.

2. One of the people ____*who(m)*____ I watched at the race track lost a huge amount of money.

3. My neighbor is a kind person _____ is always willing to help people in trouble.

4. The people _____ we visited gave us tea and a light snack.

5. The doctor _____ lives on my street is a surgeon.

6. My mother is a woman _____ I admire tremendously.

7. I thanked the man _____ helped me.

8. The woman _____ I helped thanked me.

★There are parentheses around the "m" in *who(m)* to show that, in everyday informal English, *who* may be used as an object pronoun instead of *whom*.

◇ PRACTICE 7—GUIDED STUDY: Using *who* and *who(m)* in adjective clauses. (Chart 12-2)

Directions: Complete the sentences with **WHO** or **WHO(M)**.

1. The children _____*who*_____ live down the street in the yellow house are always polite.

2. The children _____*who(m)*_____ I watched at the park were feeding ducks in a pond.

3. People _____ listen to very loud music may suffer gradual hearing loss.

4. There are many good people in the world _____ you can trust to be honest and honorable at all times.

5. Marie and Luis Escobar still keep in touch with many of the students _____ they met in their English class five years ago.

6. My husband is a person _____ enjoys good food and good friends.

7. At the supermarket yesterday, one of the store employees caught a man _____ had put a beefsteak in his coat pocket and attempted to walk out without paying.

8. The couple _____ I invited to dinner at my home were an hour late. I thought that was very rude. They didn't call. They didn't have an excuse. I'll never invite them again.

◇ PRACTICE 8—SELFSTUDY: Using *that* or Ø in adjective clauses. (Chart 12-3)

Directions: Cross out the word **THAT** if possible.

1. That man ~~that~~ I saw was wearing a black hat.
2. The people that visited us stayed too long. *(no change)*
3. The fruit that I bought today at the market is fresh.
4. My high school English teacher is a person that I will never forget.
5. The puppy that barked the loudest got the most attention in the pet store.
6. The girl that is sitting in front of Richard has long black hair that she wears in a ponytail.

◇ PRACTICE 9—SELFSTUDY: Using *who, who(m), that* and Ø in adjective clauses.
(Chart 12-3)

Directions: In the box write every possible PRONOUN that can be used to connect the adjective clause to the main clause: WHO, WHO(M), or THAT. Also, write Ø if the pronoun can be omitted.

1. The woman [**who** **that**] sat next to me on the plane talked a lot.

2. The woman [**who(m)** **that** **Ø**] I met on the plane talked a lot.

3. Three men [   ] I didn't know walked into my office.

4. The three men [   ] walked into my office were strangers.

5. My cousin's wife is the woman [   ] is talking to Mr. Horn.

6. I like the woman [   ] my brother and I visited.

◇ PRACTICE 10—SELFSTUDY: *Who* and *who(m)* vs. *which.* (Charts 12-2 → 12-4)

Directions: Choose the correct answer.

1. The magazine ___**C**___ I read on the plane was interesting.
   A. who   B. who(m)   C. which

2. The artist _____ drew my picture is very good.
   A. who   B. who(m)   C. which

3. I really enjoyed the experiences _____ I had on my trip to Nigeria.
   A. who   B. who(m)   C. which

4. Most of the games _____ we played as children no longer amuse us.
   A. who   B. who(m)   C. which

5. All of the people _____ I called yesterday can come to the meeting on Monday.
   A. who   B. who(m)   C. which

6. The teacher _____ was ill canceled her math class.
   A. who   B. who(m)   C. which

◇   PRACTICE 11—SELFSTUDY: Using *which*, *that*, and *Ø* in adjeclive clauses. (Chart 12-4)

Directions: Write the PRONOUNS that can be used to connect the adjective clause to the main clause: **WHICH** or **THAT**. Also write *Ø* if the pronoun can be omitted.

1. I really enjoyed the show | *which* *that* *Ø* | we saw last night.

2. Tim liked the show | | was playing at the Fox Theater.

3. The plane | | I took to Korea arrived on time.

4. The plane | | flew to the Gold Coast left on time.

5. The books | | Jane ordered came in the mail today.

6. Jane was glad to get the books | | came in the mail today.

◇   PRACTICE 12—SELFSTUDY: Object pronouns in adjective clauses: error analysis.
                            (Charts 12-3 → 12-4)

Directions: Find and cross out the incorrect PRONOUNS in the ADJECTIVE CLAUSES.

1. The books I bought ~~them~~ at the bookstore were expensive.
2. I like the shirt you wore it to class yesterday.
3. Amanda Jones is a person I would like you to meet her.
4. The apartment we wanted to rent it had two bedrooms.
5. My wife and I are really enjoying the TV set that we bought it for ourselves last week.
6. The woman you met her at Aunt Martha's house is a pharmacist.

◇ PRACTICE 13—GUIDED STUDY: Object pronouns in adjective clauses: error analysis. (Charts 12-3 and 12-4)

Directions: Find and cross out the incorrect PRONOUNS in the ADJECTIVE CLAUSES.

1. I enjoy the relatives I visited ~~them~~ in Mexico City last year.
2. The coffee that I drank it was cold and tasteless.
3. The tennis shoes I was wearing them in the garden got wet and muddy.
4. My cousin Ahmed is a person I've known and loved him since he was born.
5. I have a great deal of respect for the wonderful woman I married her eleven years ago.
6. Anna has a cat that it likes to catch birds.
7. The birds that Anna's cat catches them are very frightened.
8. Yesterday, Anna rescued a bird that the cat had brought it into the house. She set it free. It flew away quickly.

◇ PRACTICE 14—GUIDED STUDY: Using *who, who(m), which, that,* and Ø in adjective clauses. (Charts 12-3 and 12-4)

Directions: Write the PRONOUNS that can be used to connect the adjective clause to the main clause: **WHICH, WHO, WHO(M)** or **THAT.** Also write Ø if the pronoun can be omitted.

Example: The manager . . . fired Tom is a difficult person to work for.

→ *The manager* $\begin{Bmatrix} who \\ that \end{Bmatrix}$ *fired Tom is a difficult person to work for.*

1. The box . . . I mailed to my sister was heavy.
2. The people . . . sat in the stadium cheered for the home team.
3. The calendar . . . hangs in Paul's office has pictures of wildlife.
4. The teenagers counted the money . . . they earned at the car wash.
5. The people . . . my brother called didn't answer their phone.
6. The tree branch . . . was lying in the street was a hazard to motorists.

◇ PRACTICE 15—SELFSTUDY: Pronoun usage in adjective clauses. (Charts 12-2 → 12-4)

Directions: Choose the correct answers. NOTE: There is **more than one correct answer** for each sentence.

1. I liked the teacher _____**A, C, D**_____ I had for chemistry in high school.
   A. whom   B. which   C. that   D. Ø

2. The university scientist _____ did research in the Amazon River basin found many previously unknown species of plants.
   A. who   B. whom   C. which   D. that   E. Ø

3. The children enjoyed the sandwiches _____ Mr. Rice made for them.
   A. who   B. whom   C. which   D. that   E. Ø

4. Have you ever read any books by the author _____ the teacher mentioned in class this morning?
   A. whom   B. which   C. that   D. Ø

5. The fans _____ crowded the ballpark roared their approval.

   A. who   B. whom   C. which   D. that   E. Ø

6. Have you been to the York Art Gallery? It has a new exhibit _____ includes the work of several local artists.
   A. who   B. whom   C. which   D. that   E. Ø

7. The operation _____ the surgeon performed on my uncle was very dangerous.
   A. who   B. whom   C. which   D. that   E. Ø

8. Bricks are made of soil _____ has been placed in molds, pounded down, and dried.
   A. who   B. whom   C. which   D. that   E. Ø

◇ PRACTICE 16—GUIDED STUDY: Pronoun usage in adjective clauses. (Charts 12-2 → 12-4)

Directions: Choose the correct answers. NOTE: There is **more than one correct answer** for each sentence.

1. The actors _____**A, C, D**_____ we saw at Stratford performed out-of-doors.
   A. whom   B. which   C. that   D. Ø

2. Many of the games _____ children play teach them about the adult world.
   A. who   B. whom   C. which   D. that   E. Ø

3. When Jason arrived at the reunion, the first person _____ he encountered was Sally Sellers, one of his best friends when he was in high school.
   A. whom   B. which   C. that   D. Ø

4. The earth receives less than one-billionth of the enormous amount of heat _____ the sun produces. The rest of the sun's energy disappears into outer space.
   A. who   B. whom   C. which   D. that   E. Ø

5. Two hundred years ago, people on ships and in coastal towns greatly feared the pirates _____ sailed the South China Sea and the Gulf of Thailand.
   A. who   B. whom   C. which   D. that   E. Ø

6. Piranhas are dangerous fish _____ can tear the flesh off an animal as large as a horse in a few minutes.
   A. who   B. whom   C. which   D. that   E. Ø

7. Fire swept through an old apartment building in the center of town. I know some of the people _____ the firefighters rescued. They lost all their possessions. They were grateful simply to be alive.

        A. whom   B. which   C. that   D. Ø

8. Most of the islands in the Pacific are the tops of volcanic mountains _____ rise from the floor of the ocean.

        A. who   B. whom   C. which   D. that   E. Ø

◇ PRACTICE 17—GUIDED STUDY: Adjective clauses. (Charts 12-1 → 12-4)

Directions: Answer the questions in complete sentences. Use any appropriate pattern of ADJECTIVE CLAUSE. Use **THE** with the noun that is modified by the adjective clause.

1. We ate some food from our garden.
   We ate some food at a restaurant.
   Which food was very expensive?
   → **The** *food we ate at a restaurant was very expensive.* **The** *food we ate from our garden was not expensive at all.*

2. One phone wasn't ringing.
   The other phone was ringing.
   Which phone did Sam answer?
   → *Sam answered* **the** *phone that was ringing. He didn't answer* **the** *phone that wasn't ringing.*

3. One girl won the foot race.
   The other girl lost the foot race.
   Which girl is happy?

4. One man was sleeping.
   Another man was listening to the radio.
   One of them heard the news bulletin about the earthquake in China. Which one?

5. One person raised her hand in class.
   Another person sat quietly in his seat.
   One of them asked the teacher a question. Which one?

6. One person bought a *(brand name of a car)*.
   Another person bought a *(brand name of a car)*.
   Which person spent more money than the other?

7. Pretend I'm at the market. Some of the bananas are completely brown.
   Some of the bananas are green.
   Which bananas should I buy?

8. Amanda bought some canned vegetables at a small food store.
   Tom picked some vegetables from his grandfather's garden.
   Which vegetables tasted fresh?

9. One young musician practiced hours and hours every day.
   The other young musician had a regular job and practiced only in the evenings and on the weekends.
   Which musician showed a great deal of improvement during the course of a year?

10. One city provides clean water and a modern sewer system for its citizens.
    Another city uses its rivers and streams as both a source of water and a sewer.
    Which city has a high death rate from infectious diseases such as typhoid and cholera?

◇ PRACTICE 18—GUIDED STUDY: Adjective clauses. (Charts 12-1 → 12-4)

Directions: Complete the definitions that begin in COLUMN A with the information given in COLUMN B. Use ADJECTIVE CLAUSES in the definitions.

Example: An architect is someone who designs buildings.

COLUMN A	COLUMN B
1. An architect is someone	A. It is built for fast driving.
2. A vegetarian is a person	B. It is worn on a finger for decoration.
3. Steam is gas	C. It cannot be understood or explained.
4. A turtle is an animal	D. S/he leaves society and lives completely alone.
5. A ring is a circle of metal	E. It can be shaped and hardened to form many useful
6. An expressway is a road	things.
7. A hermit is a person	F. It grows in hot climates and produces large
8. A banana tree is a plant	bunches of yellow fruit.
9. Plastic is a synthetic material . . . . ✔ G.	S/he designs buildings.
10. A mystery is something	H. It has a hard shell and can live in water or on land.
	I. It forms when water boils.
	J. S/he doesn't eat meat.

◇ PRACTICE 19—GUIDED STUDY: Adjective clauses. (Charts 12-1 → 12-4)

Directions: In groups or pairs, provide definitions for the words listed below. Consult your dictionaries if necessary.

Example: A telephone directory is a book . . . .
→ *A telephone directory is a book that lists telephone numbers.*

1. A dictionary is a book . . . .
2. An author is someone . . . .
3. A giraffe is an animal . . . .
4. Parents are people . . . .
5. A key is a piece of metal . . . .
6. A prisoner is a person . . . .
7. Water is a substance . . . .
8. Photographers are people . . . .
9. A hero is a person . . . .
10. An adjective is a word . . . .
11. A triangle is a geometric form . . . .
12. Friends are people . . . .

◇ PRACTICE 20—SELFSTUDY: Subject-verb agreement in adjective clauses. (Chart 12-5)

Directions: Complete the sentence with the correct form of the verb in parentheses. Use the SIMPLE PRESENT. <u>Underline</u> the noun that determines whether the verb in the ADJECTIVE CLAUSE is singular or plural.

1. A saw is a <u>tool</u> that _____ **is** _____ used to cut wood. *(be)*

2. Hammers are <u>tools</u> that _____ **are** _____ used to pound nails. *(be)*

3. I recently met a woman who _____ in Montreal. *(live)*

4. Most of the people who _____ in Montreal speak French as their first language. *(live)*

5. I have a cousin who _____ as a coal miner. *(work)*

6. Some coal miners who _____ underground suffer from lung disease. *(work)*

7. A professional athlete who _____ tennis for a living is called a tennis pro. *(play)*

8. Professional athletes who _____ tennis for a living can make a lot of money. *(play)*

9. A carpenter is a person who _____ things out of wood. *(make)*

10. Sculptors are artists who _____ things from clay or other materials. *(make)*

◇ PRACTICE 21—SELFSTUDY: Prepositions in adjective clauses. (Chart 12-6)

Directions: The adjective clauses in the following sentences need PREPOSITIONS. Add the prepositions and give all the possible patterns for the ADJECTIVE CLAUSE. Write "Ø" if nothing is needed.

1. The bus _____ *that* _____ we were waiting _____ *for* _____ was an hour late.

   The bus _____ *which* _____ we were waiting _____ *for* _____ was an hour late.

   The bus _____ *Ø* _____ we were waiting _____ *for* _____ was an hour late.

   The bus _____ *for which* _____ we were waiting _____ *Ø* _____ was an hour late.

2. The music _____ I listened _____ was pleasant.

   The music _____ I listened _____ was pleasant.

   The music _____ I listened _____ was pleasant.

   The music _____ I listened _____ was pleasant.

3. Ecology is one of the subjects _____ I am very interested _____.

   Ecology is one of the subjects _____ I am very interested _____.

   Ecology is one of the subjects _____ I am very interested _____.

   Ecology is one of the subjects _____ I am very interested _____.

4. Tom argued with a man about politics.

   The man _____ Tom was arguing _____ was very angry.

   The man _____ Tom was arguing _____ was very angry.

   The man _____ Tom was arguing _____ was very angry.

   The man _____ Tom was arguing _____ was very angry.

◇ PRACTICE 22—GUIDED STUDY: Prepositions in adjective clauses. (Chart 12-6)

Directions: Complete the given sentences with PRONOUNS and PREPOSITIONS, as necessary. Give all the possible patterns for the ADJECTIVE CLAUSES.

Example: The movie . . . we went . . . was good.
   →   *The movie that we went to was good.*
       The movie which we went to was good.
       The movie Ø we went to was good.
       The movie to which we went was good.

1. I enjoyed meeting the people . . . you introduced me . . . yesterday.

2. English grammar is a subject . . . I am quite familiar . . . .

3. The woman . . . Mr. Low told us . . . works for the government.

◇ PRACTICE 23—SELFSTUDY: Prepositions in adjective clauses. (Chart 12-6)

Directions: Supply appropriate PREPOSITIONS in the blanks. Write "Ø" if no preposition is necessary. In sentence b., put brackets around the ADJECTIVE CLAUSE.

1. a. I enjoyed the CD. We listened _____ *to* _____ it at Sara's apartment.

   b. I enjoyed the CD [we listened _____ *to* _____ at Sara's apartment.]

2. a. I paid the shopkeeper for the glass cup. I accidentally broke _____ *Ø* _____ it.

   b. I paid the shopkeeper for the glass cup [I accidentally broke _____ *Ø* _____.]

3. a. The bus was only three minutes late. We were waiting _____ it.

   b. The bus we were waiting _____ was only three minutes late.

4. a. Mrs. Chan is someone. I always enjoy talking _____ her about politics.

   b. Mrs. Chan is someone I always enjoy talking _____ about politics.

5. a. I showed my roommate the letter. I had just written _____ it.

   b. I showed my roommate the letter I had just written _____.

6. a. One of the subjects is global economics. I've been interested _____ it for a long time.

   b. One of the subjects I've been interested _____ for a long time is global economics.

◇ PRACTICE 24—SELFSTUDY: Prepositions in adjective clauses. (Chart 12-6)

Directions: Put brackets around the ADJECTIVE CLAUSE in each sentence. Add an appropriate PREPOSITION, if necessary. If no preposition is needed, write "Ø."

1. The book catalogue [I was looking _____ *at* _____] had hundreds of interesting titles.

2. The book [I wanted _____ *Ø* _____] wasn't available at the library.

3. I really enjoyed the music we were listening _____ at Jim's yesterday.

4. The man I was staring _____ started to stare back at me.

5. My father is someone I've always been able to depend _____ when I need advice or help.

6. The suitcases I was carrying _____ got so heavy that my arms started to ache.

7. Organic chemistry is a subject that I'm not familiar _____.

8. The news article we talked _____ in class concerned a peace conference.

9. Chris looks angry. The man she is arguing _____ is her cousin.

10. Jennifer and David stopped at a sidewalk cafe. The food they ate _____ at the cafe was delicious.

11. The sailor you waved _____ is walking toward us. What are you going to say?

12. The bank I borrowed money _____ charges high interest on its loans.

◇ PRACTICE 25—GUIDED STUDY: Prepositions in adjective clauses. (Chart 12-6)

Directions: Put brackets around the ADJECTIVE CLAUSE in each sentence. Add an appropriate PREPOSITION, if necessary. If no preposition is needed, write "Ø."

1. The people [I talked ___*to/with*___ at the reception] were interesting.

2. One of the places [I want to visit ___*Ø*___ next year] is Mexico City.

3. My sister and I have the same ideas about almost everything. She is the one person [___*with*___ whom I almost always agree.]

4. The man _____ whom I spoke at the airline counter asked to see my passport and ticket.

5. The furniture I bought _____ was expensive.

6. What's the name of the person you introduced me _____ at the restaurant last night? I've already forgotten.

7. Botany is a subject I'm not familiar _____.

8. The bags I was carrying _____ were really heavy.

9. The guy I borrowed these tools _____ wants them back today.

10. English grammar is one of the subjects _____ which I enjoy studying the most.

11. The friend I waved _____ didn't wave back. Maybe he just didn't see me.

12. The people _____ whom Alex was waiting were over an hour late.

13. What was that tape you were just listening _____? I really liked it.

14. The newspaper I was reading _____ had the latest news about the election.

15. Your building supervisor is the person _____ whom you should complain if you have any problems with your apartment.

16. My parents are people I can always rely _____ for support and help.

17. Taking out the garbage is one of the chores our fourteen-year-old is responsible _____.

18. The interviewer wanted to know the name of the college I had graduated _____.

◇ PRACTICE 26—SELFSTUDY: Adjective clauses with *whose*. (Chart 12-7)

Directions: Find and underline the ADJECTIVE CLAUSE in the long sentence. Then change the long sentence into two short sentences.

1. *Long sentence:*   I know a man <u>whose daughter is a pilot</u>.

Short sentence 1:   ___*I know **a man**.*___

Short sentence 2:   ___**His daughter is a pilot.**___

2. *Long sentence:* The woman <u>whose husband is out of work</u> found a job at Mel's Diner.

   Short sentence 1:   *The woman* **found a job at Mel's Diner.**

   Short sentence 2:   **Her**

3. *Long sentence:* The man whose wallet I found gave me a reward.

   Short sentence 1:   *The man*

   Short sentence 2:

4. *Long sentence:* I know a girl whose family never eats dinner together.

   Short sentence 1:

   Short sentence 2:

5. *Long sentence:* The people whose window I broke got really angry.

   Short sentence 1:

   Short sentence 2:

◇ PRACTICE 27—SELFSTUDY: Adjective clauses. (Charts 12-1 → 12-7)

Directions: Use the given information to complete the sentences with ADJECTIVE CLAUSES. Omit the PRONOUN from the adjective clause if possible.

I share their views.

Their children were doing poorly in her class.

They disrupted the global climate and caused mass extinctions of animal life.

✔ *The man's son was in an accident.*

Ted bought them for his wife on their anniversary.

I slept on it at the hotel last night.

They had backbones.

✔ *James chose the color of paint for his bedroom walls.*

It is used to carry boats with goods and/or passengers.

1. The man _____*whose son was in an accident*_____ called an ambulance.

2. The color of paint_____*James chose for his bedroom walls*_____ was an unusual blue.

3. My back hurts today. The mattress _____

   was too soft.

4. A waterway is a river or stream _____.

5. The second grade teacher talked to all the parents _____

   _____.

6. The flowers _____

   wilted in the heat before he got home.

7. The candidates _____will get my votes.

8. According to scientists, the first animals _____

   were fish. They appeared on the earth about 500 million years ago.

9. Approximately 370 million years ago, seventy percent of the earth's marine species mysteriously vanished. Approximately 65 million years ago, the dinosaurs and two-thirds of all marine animal species became extinct. According to some scientific researchers, the earth was struck by speeding objects from space _____.

◇ PRACTICE 28—GUIDED STUDY: Adjective clauses. (Charts 12-1 → 12-7)

Directions: Use the given information in the list to complete the sentences with ADJECTIVE CLAUSES. Omit the OBJECT PRONOUN from the adjective clause if possible.

Their specialty is heart surgery.

Its mouth was big enough to swallow a whole cow in one gulp.

You drink it.

It erupted in Indonesia recently.

They lived in the jungles of Southeast Asia.

These molecules have been used countless times before in countless ways.

They continued week after week.

1. A volcano _____ killed six people and damaged large areas of rice, coconut, and clove crops.

2. Doctors and nurses _____ are some of the best-trained medical personnel in the world.

3. Early human beings hunted animals for food, including chickens. Originally, chickens were wild birds _____.
   At some point in time, humans learned how to domesticate them and raise them for food.

4. In prehistoric times, there was a dinosaur _____
   _____

5. Several years ago, tons of fish in the Seine River died from lack of oxygen when the river became polluted. Heavy rains _____ caused the sewer system to overflow into the river, bypassing the sewage treatment plant.

6. Every glass of water _____ has molecules
   _____.

◇ PRACTICE 29—SELFSTUDY: Adjective clauses. (Charts 12-1 → 12-7)

Directions: Which of the following can be used in the blanks: WHO, WHO(M), WHICH, THAT, WHOSE, or Ø?

1. The people _____**who/that**_____ moved into town are Italian.

2. The lamp _____ I bought downtown is beautiful and quite expensive.

3. Everyone _____ came to the audition got a part in the play.

4. Ms. Laura Rice is the teacher _____ class I enjoy most.

5. Flowers _____ grow in tropical climates usually have vibrant colors.

6. The man _____ I found in the doorway had collapsed from exhaustion.

7. Flying squirrels _____ live in tropical rain forests stay in the trees their entire lives without ever touching the ground.

8. The girl _____ skirt was caught in the classroom door seemed very embarrassed.

◇ PRACTICE 30—GUIDED STUDY: Adjective clauses. (Charts 12-1 → 12-7)

Directions: Which of the following can be used in the blanks: WHO, WHO(M), WHICH, THAT, WHOSE, or Ø?

1. What do you say to people _____*who/that*_____ ask you personal questions that you don't want to answer?

2. In my country, any person _____ is twenty-one years old or older can vote. I turned twenty-one last year. The person _____ I voted for in the national election lost. I hope the next candidate for _____ I vote has better luck. I'd like to vote for a winning candidate.

3. Vegetarians are people _____ do not eat meat. True vegetarians do not eat flesh _____ comes from any living creature, including fish. Some vegetarians even exclude any food _____ is made from animal products such as milk and eggs.

4. A: A magazine _____ I read at the doctor's office had an article _____ you ought to read. It's about the importance of exercise in dealing with stress.

   B: Why do you think I should read an article _____ deals with exercise and stress?

   A: If you stop and think for a minute, you can answer that question yourself. You're under a lot of stress, and you don't get any exercise.

   B: The stress _____ I have at work doesn't bother me. It's just a normal part of my job. And I don't have time to exercise.

   A: Well, you should make time. Anyone _____ job is as stressful as yours should make physical exercise part of a daily routine.

◇ PRACTICE 31—SELFSTUDY: Adjective clauses. (Charts 12-1 → 12-7)

Directions: Find and underline the ADJECTIVE CLAUSES in the following passages. Circle the NOUN that each adjective clause modifies.

1. (Flowers) that bloom year after year are called perennials. (Flowers) that bloom only one season are called annuals.

2. A: Who's that boy?

   B: Which boy? Are you talking about the boy who's wearing the striped shirt or the boy who has on the T-shirt?

   A: I'm not talking about either one of them. I'm talking about the boy who just waved at us. Look. Over there. Do you see the kid that has the red baseball cap?

   B: Sure. I know him. That's Al Jordan's kid. His name is Josh or Jake or Jason. Nice kid. Did you wave back?

3. Hiroki is from Japan. When he was sixteen, he spent four months in South America. He stayed with a family who lived near Quito, Ecuador. Their way of life was very different from his. At first, all of the things they did and said seemed strange to Hiroki: their eating customs, political views, ways of expressing emotion, work habits, sense of humor, and more. He felt homesick for people who were like him in their customs and habits. But as time went on, he began to appreciate the way of life that his host family followed. Many of the things Hiroki did with his host family began to feel natural to him. He developed a strong bond of friendship with them. At the beginning of his stay in Ecuador, he had noticed only the things that were different between his host family and himself. At the end, he understood how many things they had in common as human beings despite their differences in cultural backgrounds.

4. Many of the problems that exist today have existed since the beginning of recorded history. One of these problems is violent conflict between people who come from different geographical areas or cultural backgrounds. One group may distrust and fear another group of people who are different from themselves in language, customs, politics, religion, and/or appearance. These irrational fears are the source of much of the violence that has occurred throughout the history of the world.

Directions: Find and <u>underline</u> the ADJECTIVE CLAUSES in the following passage. Circle the NOUN that each adjective clause modifies.

Parents are (people) who <u>provide love, care, and education for children</u>. Parents may be defined as the principal people who raise a child. These people may or may not have physically produced the child. Many children are brought up by relatives or other caring adults when their biological parents, through death, disability or uncontrollable circumstances, are not present to care for them. The role of any parents, biological or not, is to take care of their children's emotional, physical, and social needs.

Children need love and affection to grow strong emotionally. It is important for all children to have at least one adult with whom they can form a loving, trusting relationship. A strong bond with adults is essential from birth through adolescence. For example, babies who are not picked up frequently and held lovingly may have slow physical and mental growth even though they receive adequate food and exercise. Youngsters who are raised in an institution without bonding with an older person who functions as a parent may often have difficulty forming trusting relationships when they are adults.

In addition to love, children need physical care. Babies are completely dependent upon adults for food, shelter, and safety. Children who are denied such basics in their early lives may suffer chronic health problems and feelings of insecurity throughout their lifetimes. One of the greatest responsibilities that parents have is to provide for the physical well-being of their children.

Children's education is also the responsibility of the parents. Girls and boys must learn to speak, dress themselves, eat properly, and get along with others. They must learn not to touch fire, to look carefully before they cross the street, and not to use violence to solve problems. The lessons that parents teach their children are numerous. As children get older and enter school, teachers join parents in providing the education that young people need in order to become independent, productive members of society.

◇   PRACTICE 33—GUIDED STUDY: Adjective clauses. (Chapter 12)

> Directions: Discuss or write about the following topics. Incorporate ADJECTIVE CLAUSES into sentences whenever possible.

1. What are the qualities of a friend?
2. What kind of neighbors do you like to have?
3. What kind of people make good leaders?
4. What kind of people make good parents?
5. What is your idea of the ideal roommate?
6. What qualities do you expect in a boss?
7. What is one of the things you enjoy most about living here?
8. What is one of the things you dislike about living here?
9. Describe your dream house.
10. Describe your ideal vacation.

◇   PRACTICE 34—SELFSTUDY: Phrasal verbs. (Chart 12-8)

> Directions: Complete the sentences with the given PARTICLES.

down	*in*	*off*	*out*	*over*	*up*

1. If I quit a bad habit like smoking, that means I give it _____**up**_____.

2. If I don't want to include something when I write a letter, I leave it _____.

3. When I write words in this practice, I am filling _____ the blanks.

4. When I discover new information, that means I find something _____.

5. Sometimes when I recite a poem, I forget a line. So I go back to the beginning and start

   _____.

6. When buildings are old and dangerous, we tear them _____.

7. If I write a letter and I don't like what I've written, I will write it again. That means I'll do it

   _____.

8. When I remove a piece of paper from a spiral notebook, I tear the paper _____ of

   my notebook.

9. When I write something that I don't want anybody else to see, I tear the paper into tiny pieces.

   I tear _____ the note.

10. When I write information on an application form, I fill the form _____.

11. When I make a mistake in something I write, I erase the mistake if I'm using a pencil. If I'm

    using a pen, I cross the mistake _____ by drawing a line through it.

12. When my tea cup is empty, I fill it _____ again if I'm still thirsty.

◇ PRACTICE 35—SELFSTUDY: Phrasal verbs. (Chart 12-9)

Directions: Complete each sentence with **two** PARTICLES.

1. When I cross a busy street, I'm careful. I look _____*out*_____ _____*for*_____ cars and trucks.

2. Some friends visited me last night. I hadn't expected them. They just dropped _____ _____ me.

3. Maria was born and raised in Brazil. in other words, she grew _____ _____ Brazil.

4. If I like people and enjoy their company, that means I get _____ _____ them.

5. My cousin never does anything useful. He just fools _____ _____ his friends all day wasting time.

6. When somebody uses the last spoonful of sugar in the kitchen, we don't have any more sugar. That means we have run _____ _____ sugar and need to go to the market.

7. I'm glad when I finish my homework. When I get _____ _____ my homework, I can go out and play tennis or do whatever else I feel like doing.

8. In some places, it's important to be careful about pickpockets. There are places where tourists have to watch _____ _____ pickpockets.

9. If you return from a trip, that means you get _____ _____ a trip.

10. Sometimes students have to quit school because they need to get a job, fail their courses, or lose interest in their education. There are various reasons why students drop _____ _____ school.

CHAPTER 13
Comparisons

◇ PRACTICE 1—SELFSTUDY: *As . . . as.* (Chart 13-1)

Directions: Using the given information and the words in parentheses, complete the comparisons using **AS . . . AS.** Use **NOT** with the verb as necessary.

1. Dogs make more noise than cats do. *(be noisy)*

   → Cats _____**aren't as noisy as**_____ dogs.

2. Both Anne and her sister Amanda are lazy. *(be lazy)*

   → Anne _____**is as lazy as**_____ her sister Amanda.

3. Adults have more strength than children. *(be strong)*

   → Children _____ adults.

4. Tom and Jerry are the same height. *(be tall)*

   → Tom _____ Jerry.

5. It's more comfortable to live at home than in a dormitory. *(be comfortable)*

   → Living in a dormitory _____ living at home.

6. Both the bride and the groom were nervous before the wedding. *(be nervous)*

   → The bride _____ the groom.

7. A basketball is bigger than a soccer ball. *(be big)*

   → A soccer ball _____ a basketball.

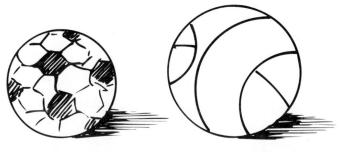

SOCCER BALL   BASKETBALL

8. The air in a big city is more polluted than the air in the countryside. *(be fresh and clean)*

    → The air in a big city _____ the air in the countryside.

9. My sister wants to be a famous and successful businesswoman. I don't have any plans for my

    future. *(be ambitious)*

    → I _____ my sister.

10. Some school subjects interest me, and others don't. *(be interesting)*

    → Some school subjects _____ others.

◇ PRACTICE 2—SELFSTUDY: *As . . . as.* (Chart 13-1)

Directions: Complete the sentences with one of the following:

> *just as*
> *almost as/not quite as*
> *not nearly as*

PART I: Compare the boxes.

1. Box B is _____**almost as / not quite as**_____ big as Box A.

2. Box E is _____ big as Box A.

3. Box C is _____ big as Box B.

4. Box E is _____ big as Box D.

PART II: Meeting time: 9:00 A.M. Compare the arrival times.

Arrival times:
David	9:01 A.M.
Julia	9:14 A.M.
Laura	9:15 A.M.
Paul	9:15 A.M.
James	9:25 A.M.

5. Paul was _____ late as Laura.

6. David was _____ late as James.

7. Julia was _____ late as Laura.

8. Julia was _____ late as Paul.

PART III: Compare world temperatures today.

Bangkok	92°F/33°C
Cairo	85°F/30°C
Madrid	90°F/32°C
Moscow	68°F/20°C
Tokyo	85°F/30°C

9. Tokyo is _____ hot as Cairo.

10. Moscow is _____ hot as Bangkok.

11. Madrid is _____ hot as Bangkok.

PART IV: Compare world temperatures yesterday and today.

	Yesterday	*Today*
Bangkok	95°F/35°C	92°F/33°C
Cairo	95°F/35°C	85°F/30°C
Madrid	90°F/32°C	90°F/32°C
Moscow	70°F/21°C	68°F/20°C
Tokyo	81°F/27°C	85°F/30°C

12. Cairo was _____ hot as Bangkok yesterday.

13. It's _____ warm in Moscow today as yesterday.

14. Madrid is _____ hot today as yesterday.

15. It was _____ hot in Tokyo yesterday as in Bangkok.

16. It's _____ hot in Bangkok today as yesterday.

◇ PRACTICE 3—GUIDED STUDY: *As . . . as.* (Chart 13-1)

Directions: Complete the sentences with your own words.

Example: . . . not as sharp as . . . .
  → *A pencil point isn't as sharp as a needle.*
  → *A kitchen knife isn't as sharp as a razor blade.*
  → *My mind isn't as sharp in the afternoon as it is in the morning.*

1. . . . just as important as . . . .
2. . . . not as comfortable as . . . .
3. . . . not nearly as interesting as . . . .
4. . . . just as good as . . . .
5. . . . not quite as difficult as . . . .
6. . . . not as quiet as . . . .
7. . . . almost as good as . . . .
8. . . . not as friendly as . . . .
9. . . . not as heavy as . . . .
10. . . . just as soft as . . . .

◇ PRACTICE 4—SELFSTUDY: *As . . . as.* (Chart 13-1)

Directions: Choose the best sentence completion from the given list.

A. *as bad as she said it was*   ✔E. *as much as possible*
B. *as easy as it looks*   F. *as often as I can*
C. *as fast as I could*   G. *as often as I used to*
D. *as good as they looked*   H. *us soon as possible*

1. I have a lot of homework. I will finish ____**E**____ before I go to bed.

2. I'm sorry I'm late. I drove _____.

3. I saw some chocolates at the candy store. They looked delicious, so I bought some. They tasted just _____.

4. When I was in college, I went to at least two movies every week. Now I'm very busy with my job and family, so I don't go to movies _____.

5. It took Julie years of lessons to be able to play the piano well. She makes it look easy, but we all know that playing a musical instrument isn't _____.

6. I need to finish working on this report, so go ahead and start the meeting without me. I'll be there _____.

7. Even though I'm very busy, I'm usually just sitting at my desk all day. I need more exercise, so I try to walk to and from work _____.

8. My friend told me the movie was terrible, but I went anyway. My friend was right. The movie was just _____.

◇ PRACTICE 5—SELFSTUDY: Comparative and superlative forms. (Chart 13-3)

Directions: Give the COMPARATIVE and SUPERLATIVE forms of the words below.

	COMPARATIVE			SUPERLATIVE	
1. strong	*stronger*	than	the	*strongest*	of all
2. important	*more important*	than	the	*most important*	of all
3. soft	_____	than	the	_____	of all
4. lazy	_____	than	the	_____	of all
5. wonderful	_____	than	the	_____	of all
6. calm	_____	than	the	_____	of all
7. tame	_____	than	the	_____	of all
8. dim	_____	than	the	_____	of all
9. convenient	_____	than	the	_____	of all
10. clever	_____	than	the	_____	of all
11. good	_____	than	the	_____	of all

12. bad   _____ than   the _____ of all

13. far   _____ than   the _____ of all

14. slow   _____ than   the _____ of all

15. slowly   _____ than   the _____ of all

◇ PRACTICE 6—GUIDED STUDY: Comparative and superlative forms. (Charts 13-2 and 13-3)

Directions: As a class or in smaller groups, divide into two teams. Each team will try to score points by (1) giving the meaning of an adjective and (2) giving its comparative and superlative forms. (3) Bonus points will be awarded for every correct sentence the team creates using the comparative or superlative of the given adjective.

Each team has thirty seconds or a minute (or any other agreed upon length of time) for each word. (Someone in the class needs to be the timekeeper.) The teams should prepare for the contest by discussing the words in the list, looking them up in the dictionary if necessary, and making up possible sentences.

SCORING:
(1) one point for the correct *meaning* of the given adjective
(2) one point for the correct *comparative and superlative forms* of that adjective
(3) one point for each clear *sentence* with the correct comparative or superlative form

Example: dependable

LEADER: What does "dependable" mean?

TEAM: "Dependable" means "responsible, reliable, trustworthy." For example, it describes people who do their jobs well every day.

LEADER: Yes. That's one point. Now, comparative and superlative forms?

TEAM: More dependable than, the most dependable of all.

LEADER: Correct. That's one point. Sentences?

TEAM: Adults are more dependable than children.

LEADER: Good. One point.

TEAM: Vegetables are more dependable than fruit.

LEADER: What? That doesn't make any sense. No point.

TEAM: My parents always support me. They are the most dependable people I know.

LEADER: Great sentence! One point.—Time is up. Your total points as a team: Four.

List of adjectives:

1. wonderful	8. heavy	15. bright
2. high	9. dangerous	16. pleasant
3. easy	10. humid	17. polite
4. intelligent	11. confusing	18. soft
5. calm	12. clever	19. sour
6. dim	13. fresh	20. common
7. wild	14. friendly	

◇ PRACTICE 7—SELFSTUDY: Comparatives. (Charts 13-2 and 13-3)

Directions: Complete the sentences with the correct COMPARATIVE form (MORE/-ER) of the given adjectives.

bad	cold	funny	pretty
careful	confusing	generous	✔ soft
clean	expensive	lazy	thin

1. I like to sit on pillows. They are a lot _____ *softer* _____ than a hardwood seat.

2. The average temperature in Moscow is _____ than the average temperature in Hong Kong.

3. This gold ring costs much more than that silver one. Can you tell me why gold is _____ than silver?

4. Bobby! How did you get all covered with mud? Hurry and take a bath. Even the floor is _____ than you are.

5. Fresh flowers not only smell good, but they're a lot _____ than artificial flowers.

6. Sandy, when you drive to the airport today, you have to be _____ than you were the last time you went. You almost had an accident because you weren't paying attention to your driving.

7. I heard a little polite laughter when I told my jokes, but everyone laughed loudly when Janet was telling hers. Her jokes are always much _____ than mine.

8. I have trouble understanding Professor Larson. Her lectures are much _____ than Professor Sato's.

9. Your father seems to give you plenty of money for living expenses. He is _____ than mine.

10. My handwriting isn't very good, but my wife's handwriting is practically illegible. Her handwriting is much _____ than mine.

11. Cardboard has thickness, but paper doesn't. Paper is _____ than cardboard.

12. I don't like to work hard, but my sister does. I'm a lot _____ than my sister.

◇ PRACTICE 8—GUIDED STUDY: Comparatives. (Charts 13-2 and 13-3)

Directions: Complete the sentences with the correct COMPARATIVE form (MORE/-ER) of the given adjectives and adverbs.

comfortable	*expensive*	*softly*
dangerous	*friendly*	✔ *sweet*
dark	*slowly*	*wet*

1. Lemons aren't _____ **sweeter** _____ than oranges. Lemons are sour.

2. Refrigerators cost a lot. They are much _____ than microwave ovens.

3. Children seem to be able to appear out of nowhere. When I'm near a school, I always drive

   _____ than I have to.

4. In my experience, old shoes are usually a lot _____ than new shoes.

5. People in villages seem to be _____ than people in large cities. They

   seem to enjoy talking to strangers.

6. Babies don't like loud noises. Most people speak _____ than usual when

   they're talking to a baby.

7. Many more people die in car accidents than in plane accidents. Statistics show that driving

   your own car is _____ than flying in an airplane.

8. A: Why does wet sand look _____ than dry sand?

   B: Because wet sand reflects less light.

9. If a cat and a duck are out in the rain, the cat will get much _____ than

   the duck. The water will simply roll off of the duck's feathers but will soak into the cat's fur.

◇ PRACTICE 9—SELFSTUDY: *Farther* and *further*. (Chart 13-3)

> Directions: Choose the correct answer or answers. **Both** answers may be correct.

1. Ron and his friend went jogging. Ron ran two miles, but his friend got tired after one mile. Ron ran __**A, B**__ than his friend did.
   A. farther   B. further

2. If you have any ___**B**___ questions, don't hesitate to ask.
   A. farther   B. further

3. The planet Earth is _____ from the sun than the planet Mercury is.
   A. farther   B. further

4. I like my new apartment, but it is _____ away from school than my old apartment is.
   A. farther   B. further

5. Thank you for your help, but I'll be fine now. I don't want to cause you any _____ trouble.
   A. farther   B. further

6. I have no _____ need of this equipment. I'm going to sell it.
   A. farther   B. further

7. Paris is _____ north than Tokyo.
   A. farther   B. further

8. A: Mr. President, will you describe your new plans for the economy?
   B: I have no _____ comment. This press conference is over.
   A. farther   B. further

9. I'm tired. I walked _____ than I should have.
   A. farther   B. further

10. I gave my old typewriter to my younger sister because I had no _____ use for it.
    A. farther   B. further

◇ PRACTICE 10—GUIDED STUDY: Comparatives. (Charts 13-2 and 13-3)

> Directions: Choose any appropriate adjective from the list (or any adjective of your own choosing) to make comparisons of the given items. Use the COMPARATIVE form (**MORE/-ER**).

bright	*fast*	*relaxing*	*thick*
easy	*flexible*	*shallow*	*thin*
enjoyable	*heavy*	*short*	*wide and deep*

1. traveling by air/traveling by bus
   → *Traveling by air is faster than traveling by bus.*
   Traveling by air is easier than traveling by bus. (Etc.)

2. a pool/a lake

3. an elephant's neck/a giraffe's neck

4. sunlight/moonlight

5. iron/wood

6. walking/running

7. river/stream

8. rubber/wood

9. nothing/sitting in a garden on a quiet summer day

10. a butterfly's wing/a blade of grass

◇ PRACTICE 11—SELFSTUDY: Completing comparisons with pronouns. (Chart 13-4)

Directions: Complete the comparisons with a PRONOUN and an appropriate AUXILIARY VERB.

1. Bob arrived at ten. I arrived at eleven.

   → Bob arrived earlier than _____ **I did** _____.

2. Linda is a good painter. Steven is better.

   → He is a better painter than _____ **she is** _____.

3. Alex knows a lot of people. I don't know many people at all.

   → He knows a lot more people than _____.

4. I won the race. Patty came in second.

   → I ran faster than _____.

5. My parents were nervous about my motorcycle ride. I was just a little nervous.

   → They were a lot more nervous than _____.

6. My aunt will stay with us for two weeks. My uncle has to return home to his job after a couple of days.

   → She will be here with us a lot longer than _____.

7. Ms. Ross speaks clearly. Mr. Mudd mumbles.

   → She speaks a lot more clearly than _____.

8. I've been here for two years. Sam has been here for two months.

   → I've been here a lot longer than _____.

9. I had a good time at the picnic yesterday. Mary didn't enjoy it.

   → I had a lot more fun at the picnic than _____.

10. I can reach the top shelf of the bookcase. Tim can only reach the shelf next to the top.

    → I can reach higher than _____.

◇ PRACTICE 12—GUIDED STUDY: Unclear comparisons. (Chart 13-3)

Directions: The following are unclear comparisons. Discuss the possible meanings.

1. UNCLEAR: Ann likes her dog better than her husband.
   POSSIBLE MEANINGS:
   → *Ann likes her dog better than her husband does.*
   (Meaning: *Ann likes her dog better than her husband likes her dog.*)
   → *Ann likes her dog better than she does her husband.*
   (Meaning: *Ann likes her dog better than she likes her husband.*)

2. UNCLEAR: I know John better than Mary.

3. UNCLEAR: Sam likes football better than his wife.

4. UNCLEAR: Frank helps me more than Debra.

5. UNCLEAR: I pay my plumber more than my dentist.

◇ PRACTICE 13—SELFSTUDY: *Very* vs. *a lot/much/far*. (Chart 13-4)

Directions: Circle the correct answer or answers. **More than one** answer may be correct.

1. This watch is not _____ expensive.
   (A.) very   B. a lot   C. much   D. far

2. That watch is _____ more expensive than this one.
   A. very   (B.) a lot   (C.) much   (D.) far

3. My nephew is _____ polite.
   A. very   B. a lot   C. much   D. far

4. My nephew is _____ more polite than my niece.
   A. very   B. a lot   C. much   D. far

5. Simon is _____ taller than George.
   A. very   B. a lot   C. much   D. far

6. Simon is _____ tall.
   A. very   B. a lot   C. much   D. far

7. I think astronomy is _____ more interesting than geology.
   A. very   B. a lot   C. much   D. far

8. I think astronomy is _____ interesting.
   A. very   B. a lot   C. much   D. far

◇ PRACTICE 14—SELFSTUDY: *Less . . . than* and *not as . . . as*. (Chart 13-4)

Directions: Circle the correct answer or answers.

1. My nephew is _____ ambitious _____ my niece.
   (A.) less . . . than   (B.) not as . . . as

2. My nephew is _____ old _____ my niece.
   A. less . . . than   (B.) not as . . . as

3. A bee is _____ big _____ a bird.
   A. less . . . than   B. not as . . . as

4. Money is _____ important _____ good health.
   A. less . . . than   B. not as . . . as

5. The last exercise was _____ difficult _____ this one.
   A. less . . . than   B. not as . . . as

6. My brother is _____ interested in planning for the future _____ I am.
   A. less . . . than   B. not as . . . as

7. I am _____ good at repairing things _____ Diane is.
   A. less . . . than   B. not as . . . as

8. Some students are _____ serious about their schoolwork _____ others.
   A. less . . . than   B. not as . . . as

◇ PRACTICE 15—GUIDED STUDY: Completing a comparative. (Chart 13-4)

Directions: Answer the questions. Begin your answer with **"Yes, I've never . . . ."** Use COMPARATIVES (**MORE/-ER**) in your answer.

Example: Your friend told a story at the party last night. Was it funny?
→ *Yes, I've never heard a funnier story.* *

1. You took a test yesterday. Was it difficult?
2. You read a book that you liked very much. Was it a good book?
3. Someone said something bad to you. Were you angry?
4. I hope you liked staying in our guest room. Were you comfortable?
5. You've been carrying things and moving furniture all day. Are you tired?
6. Congratulations on the birth of your daughter. Are you happy?
7. You have known many people in your lifetime, but one person is special. Is this person kind? Is this person considerate? Is this person generous? wise? compassionate?
8. You have had many good experiences in your lifetime, but you remember one in particular. Was it an interesting experience? Was it a good experience? exciting? memorable?

◇ PRACTICE 16—SELFSTUDY: Adjectives vs. adverbs in the comparative. (Chart 13-4)

Directions: Complete each sentence using the COMPARATIVE + the correct ADJECTIVE or ADVERB. If it is an adjective, circle ADJ. If it is an adverb, circle ADV.

1. *slow* / *slowly*   I like to drive fast, but my brother William doesn't. As a rule, he drives _____ *more slowly* _____ than I do.   ADJ (ADV)

2. *slow* / *slowly*   Alex is a _____ *slower* _____ driver than I am.   (ADJ) ADV

3. *serious* / *seriously*   Some workers are _____ about their jobs than others.   ADJ   ADV

4. *serious* / *seriously*   Some workers approach their jobs _____ than others.   ADJ   ADV

5. *polite* / *politely*   Why is it that my children behave _____ at other people's houses than at home?   ADJ   ADV

6. *polite* / *politely*   Why are they _____ at Mrs. Miranda's house than at home?   ADJ   ADV

7. *careful* / *carefully*   I'm a cautious person when I express my opinions, but my sister will say anything to anyone. I'm much _____ when I speak to others than my sister is.   ADJ   ADV

---

*The understood completion of the comparison is: *I've never heard a funnier story **in my lifetime than the story my friend told at the party last night**.*

8. *careful*
   carefully
   I always speak _____ in public than my sister
   does.   **ADJ   ADV**

9. *clear*
   clearly
   I can't understand Mark's father very well when he talks, but I
   can understand Mark. He speaks much _____ than
   his father.   **ADJ   ADV**

10. *clear*
    clearly
    Mark is a much _____ speaker than his
    father.   **ADJ   ADV**

◇ PRACTICE 17—SELFSTUDY: Nouns in the comparative. (Chart 13-5)

Directions: Choose from the given words to complete the sentences with the COMPARATIVE
(**MORE/-ER**). If the word you use in the comparative is an adjective, circle ADJ. If it is an adverb,
circle ADV. If it is a noun, circle NOUN.

books	*friends*	✔ *newspapers*
carefully	*homework*	*pleasant*
easily	*loud*	*snow*

1. My husband always wants to know everything that is going on in the world. He reads many
   ___***more newspapers***___ than I do.   **ADJ   ADV   (NOUN)**

2. University students study hard. They have a lot _____ than high
   school students.   **ADJ   ADV   NOUN**

3. There is far _____ in winter in Alaska than there is in Texas.
   ADJ   ADV   NOUN

4. I'm lonely. I wish I had _____ to go places with and spend time
   with.   **ADJ   ADV   NOUN**

5. A warm, sunny day is _____ than a cold, windy day.
   ADJ   ADV   NOUN

6. Don picks up languages with little difficulty. For me, learning a second language is slow and
   difficult. I guess some people just learn languages a lot _____ than
   others.   **ADJ   ADV   NOUN**

7. The New York City Public Library has many _____ than the
   public library in Portland, Oregon.   **ADJ   ADV   NOUN**

8. I have been driving _____ since my accident.   **ADJ   ADV   NOUN**

9. Karen doesn't need a microphone when she speaks to the audience. She's the only person I
   know whose voice is _____ than mine.   **ADJ   ADV   NOUN**

◇ PRACTICE 18—GUIDED STUDY: Making comparisons: *as . . . as* and *more/-er.*
(Charts 13-1 → 13-4)

Directions: Compare the following. Use **AS . . . AS, LESS,** and **MORE/-ER.** How many points of comparison can you think of?

Example: the sun and the moon

→ *The sun is larger than the moon.*
The sun is hotter than the moon.
The sun is more important to life on earth than the moon is.
The sun is much brighter than the moon.
The moon is closer to the earth than the sun is.
The moon is less important than the sun.
The moon isn't as far away as the sun.

1. two stores in this city
2. two seasons
3. two kinds of music
4. fingers and toes
5. two classes
6. two restaurants in this city
7. iron and aluminum (American English)/aluminium (British English)
8. a cloudy day and a sunny day

◇ PRACTICE 19—SELFSTUDY: Repeating a comparative. (Chart 13-6)

Directions: Complete the sentences by REPEATING A COMPARATIVE. Use the words in the list.

angry	✔ fast	hard
big	good	weak
cold		wet

1. When I get excited, my heart beats _____**faster**_____ and _____**faster**_____.

2. I was really mad! I got _____ and _____ until my sister

   touched my arm and told me to calm down.

3. When you blow up a balloon, it gets _____ and _____.

4. As we continued traveling north, the weather got _____ and

   _____. Eventually, everything we saw was frozen.

5. My English is improving. It is getting _____ and _____

   every day.

6. As I continued walking in miserable weather, it rained _____ and
   _____. I got _____ and _____. By the time
   I got home, I was completely soaked.

7. As I continued to row the boat, my arms got _____ and
   _____ until I had almost no strength left in them at all.

◇ PRACTICE 20—SELFSTUDY: Double comparatives. (Chart 13-7)

Directions: Complete the sentences with DOUBLE COMPARATIVES (THE MORE/-ER . . .
THE MORE/-ER).

1. If the fruit is *fresh,* it tastes *good.*

   → _____**The fresher**_____ the fruit is, _____*the better*_____ it tastes.

2. We got *close* to the fire. We felt *warm.*

   → _____ we got to the fire, _____ we felt.

3. If a knife is *sharp,* it is *easy* to cut something with.

   → _____ a knife (is), _____ it is to cut

   something.

4. The party got *noisy* next door. I got *angry.*

   → I had a terrible time getting to sleep last night. My neighbors were having a loud party.

   _____ it got, _____ I got. Finally, I banged

   on the wall and told them to be quiet.

5. Bill talked very *fast.* I became *confused.*

   → Bill was trying to explain some complicated physics problems to me to help me prepare for

   an exam. He kept talking faster and faster. _____ he talked,

   _____ I became.

◇ PRACTICE 21—SELFSTUDY: Superlatives (Chart 13-8)

Directions: Complete the sentences in COLUMN A with the ideas in COLUMN B. Use the SUPERLATIVE of the adjective in parentheses. If you don't know the right answer, guess.

Example: Kangaroos are the most familiar Australian grassland animals.

COLUMN A	COLUMN B
1. Kangaroos . . .	A. (large) eyes of all four-legged land animals
2. Giraffes . . .	B. (large) ears of all animals
3. Apes and monkeys . . .	C. (long) necks of all animals
4. Bottle-nosed dolphins . . .	✔ D. (familiar) Australian grassland animals
5. African elephants . . .	E. (intelligent) animals that live in water
6. Horses . . .	F. (intelligent) animals that live on land (besides human beings)

◇ PRACTICE 22—SELFSTUDY: Superlatives. (Chart 13-8)

Directions: Use the given phrases to complete the sentences with SUPERLATIVES.

big bird   long river in South America
clean air   popular forms of entertainment
✔ deep ocean   three common street names
high mountains on earth   two great natural dangers
large living animal

1. The Pacific is _____ **the deepest ocean** _____ in the world.

2. There is almost no air pollution at the South Pole. The South Pole has _____

_____ in the world.

3. _____ are in the Himalayan Range in Asia.

4. Most birds are small, but not the flightless North African ostrich. It is _____

_____ in the world.

5. _____ to ships are fog and icebergs.

6. One of _____ throughout the

world is the motion picture.

7. _____ in the United States are

Park, Washington, and Maple.

8. _____ in South America is the

Amazon.

9. The blue whale is huge. It is _____ in the world.

Directions: Complete the sentences with SUPERLATIVES and the appropriate PREPOSITION, IN or OF.

1. Jack is *lazy*. He is _____*the laziest*_____ student ____*in*____ the class.

2. Mike and Julie were *nervous*, but Amanda was _____*the most nervous of*_____ all.

3. Costa Rico is *beautiful*. It is one of _____ countries _____ the world.

4. Scott got a *bad* score on the test. It was one of _____ scores _____ the whole school.

5. Pluto is *far* from the sun. In fact, it is _____ planet from the sun _____ our solar system.

6. There are a lot of *good* cooks in my family, but my mom is _____ cook _____ all.

7. Alaska is *big*. It is _____ _____ state _____ the United States.

8. My grandfather is very *old*. He is _____ person _____ the town where he lives.

9. That chair in the corner is *comfortable*. It is _____ chair _____ the room.

10. Everyone who ran in the race was *exhausted*, but I was _____ _____ all.

Directions: Complete the sentences with an appropriate SUPERLATIVE and the PRESENT PERFECT of the words in parentheses.

1. I have had many *good* experiences. Of those, my trip to Honduras was one of ____*the best*____ experiences I *(have, ever)* _____*have ever had*_____.

2. I know many *responsible* people. Maria is one of ___*the most responsible*___ people I *(know, ever)* _____*have ever known*_____.

3. I've had many *nice* times, but my birthday party was one of _____ times I *(have, ever)* _____.

4. I've taken many *difficult* courses, but statistics is _____ course I *(take, ever)* _____.

5. I've tasted a lot of *good* coffee, but this is _____ coffee I *(have, ever)* _____.

6. I've made a lot of *bad* mistakes in my life, but I'm afraid lending my cousin a lot of money was

_____ mistake I *(make, ever)* _____.

7. There are many *beautiful* buildings in the world, but the Taj Mahal is one of _____

_____ buildings I *(see, ever)* _____.

8. A: How do you think you did on the exam this morning?

B: I think I did pretty well. It was an *easy* test. In fact, it was one of _____

exams I *(take, ever)* _____.

◇ **PRACTICE 25—GUIDED STUDY: Completing superlatives with adjective clauses. (Chart 13-8)**

Directions: Create sentences with ONE OF plus a SUPERLATIVE and your own words. Use the following patterns:

> PATTERN A: **ONE OF + SUPERLATIVE + PLURAL NOUN + IS**
> PATTERN B: **IS + ONE OF + SUPERLATIVE + PLURAL NOUN**

Example: There are many good students in this class. Who is one of the best?
→ PATTERN A: **One of the best students** in this class **is** (Nazir).   OR
→ PATTERN B: (Nazir) **is one of the best students** in this class.

Example: You have known many interesting people. Who is one of the most interesting you've known?
→ PATTERN A: **One of the most interesting people** I've ever known **is** (Ms. Lee).   OR
→ PATTERN B: (Ms. Lee) **is one of the most interesting people** I've ever known.

1. There are many beautiful countries in the world. What is one of them?
2. There are many famous people in the world. Who is one of them?
3. There are many long rivers in the world. What is one of them?
4. You've seen some good movies. What is one of the best movies you've seen recently?
5. Have you seen any bad movies? What is one of them?
6. You've visited some interesting cities. What is one of them?
7. You know some wonderful people. Who is one of them?
8. Have you ever taken any difficult classes? What is one of them?
9. You have had many good experiences. What is one of the best experiences you've ever had?
10. There are a lot of interesting animals in the world. What is one of them?
11. What is one of the strangest things you've ever seen?
12. There are many important people in your life among your family, friends, teachers, co-workers, and others. Who is one of these people?
13. Who is one of the most important people in world politics or the history of your country?
14. Think of some happy days in your life. What was one of them?
15. Talk about one of the best trips you've taken, the funniest things you've seen, the most exciting things you've done, the easiest jobs you've had, the coldest places you've been, the best times you've had, the most decent people you've known.

◇ PRACTICE 26—SELFSTUDY: Comparatives and superlatives. (Charts 13-2 → 13-4 and 13-8)

Directions: Complete with BETTER, THE BEST, WORSE, or THE WORST.

1. I just finished a terrible book. It's _____*the worst*_____ book I've ever read.

2. The weather was bad yesterday, but it's terrible today. The weather is

_____*worse*_____ today than it was yesterday.

3. This cake is really good. It's _____ cake I've ever eaten.

4. My grades this term are great. They're much _____ than last term.

5. Being separated from my family in time of war is one of _____

experiences I can imagine.

6. I broke my nose in a football game yesterday. Today it's very painful. For some reason, the

pain is _____ today than it was yesterday.

7. The fire spread and burned down an entire city block. It was _____ fire

we've ever had in our town.

8. I think my cold is almost over. I feel a lot _____ than I did yesterday. I

can finally breathe again.

◇ PRACTICE 27—GUIDED STUDY: Comparatives and superlatives. (Charts 13-1 → 13-8)

Directions: Ask and answer questions with COMPARATIVES and SUPERLATIVES.
STUDENT A: Ask a question that uses either a comparative or a superlative.
STUDENT B: Answer the question. Use complete sentences.

Example: what . . . sweet
STUDENT A: *What is sweeter than sugar?*
STUDENT B: *Nothing is sweeter than sugar.*

Example: what . . . dangerous
STUDENT A: *What is more dangerous than riding a motorcycle without a helmet?*
STUDENT B: *Climbing a mountain without a safety rope is more dangerous than riding a motorcycle without a helmet.*

Example: who is . . . wonderful
STUDENT A: *Who is the most wonderful person you've ever known?*
STUDENT B: *That's a hard question. Probably my mother is the most wonderful person I've ever known.*

1. what is . . . important
2. who is . . . famous
3. what is . . . good
4. what is . . . bad
5. whose hair is . . . long
6. what is . . . interesting
7. which car is . . . expensive
8. what country is . . . near
9. what is . . . dangerous
10. who is . . . old
11. what is . . . beautiful
12. who is . . . kind

◇ PRACTICE 28—GUIDED STUDY: *As . . . as, more/-er, most/-est.* (Charts 13-1 → 13-8)

Directions: Complete comparisons for the following three parts.

PART I: Compare the cost of the listed items. Use the given expressions.

ITEMS TO COMPARE:

a telephone
a pencil
a pair of socks
a motorcycle

1. is less expensive than

A telephone is less expensive than a motorcycle.
A pencil is less expensive than a pair of socks.
Etc.

2. is much more expensive than
3. is not as expensive as
4. are more expensive than
5. are both less expensive than
6. is not nearly as expensive as
7. are all more expensive than

PART II: Compare the waterfalls by using the given expressions.

8. much higher
9. almost as high
10. highest
11. not nearly as high
12. not quite as high

Waterfalls of the World

Niagara Falls	Giessbach Falls	Cuquenán Falls	Angel Falls
United States and Canada	Switzerland	Venezuela	Venezuela
53 meters	604 meters	610 meters	807 meters

PART III: Compare the weight of the listed items. Use the given expressions.

ITEMS TO COMPARE:

water
iron
wood
air

13. heavier
14. lighter
15. heaviest
16. not as heavy
17. lightest
18. not nearly as light
19. both heavier

◇ PRACTICE 29—SELFSTUDY: Review of comparatives and superlatives. (Charts 13-2 → 13-8)

Directions: Complete the sentences. Use any appropriate form of the words in parentheses and add any other necessary words. There may be more than one possible completion.

1. Lead is a very heavy metal. It is *(heavy)* ___**heavier than**___ gold or silver. It is

   one of *(heavy)* ___**the heaviest**___ metals ___**of**___ all

2. Dogs are usually *(friendly)* _____ cats.

3. One of *(famous)* _____ volcanoes _____ the world is

   Mount Etna in Sicily.

4. A car has two *(wheels)* _____ a bicycle.

5. Mrs. Cook didn't ask the children to clean up the kitchen. It was *(easy)* _____

   for her to do it herself _____ to nag them to do it.

6. Duck eggs and chicken eggs are different. Duck eggs are *(large)* _____

   chicken eggs. Also, the yolk of a duck egg is *(dark)* _____ yellow

   _____ the yolk of a chicken egg.

7. One of *(safe)* _____ places to be during a lightning storm is inside a car.

8. Small birds have a much *(fast)* _____ heartbeat _____ large birds.

9. Are your feet exactly the same size? Almost everyone's left foot is *(big)* _____

   their right foot.★

10. The volcanic explosion of Krakatoa near Java in 1883 may have been *(loud)* _____

    noise _____ recorded history. It was heard 2,760 miles (4,441 kilometers) away.

★ Grammar note: In formal English, a singular pronoun is used to refer to *everyone*:
   Almost **everyone's** left foot is bigger than **his or her** right foot.
In everyday informal usage, a plural pronoun is frequently used:
   Almost **everyone's** left foot is bigger than **their** right foot.

11. In terms of area, *(large)* _____ state _____ the United States is Alaska, but it has one of *(small)* _____ populations _____ all the states.

12. Nothing is *(important)* _____ good health. Certainly gaining wealth is much *(important)* _____ enjoying good health.

13. I need more facts. I can't make my decision until I get *(information)* _____.

14. Rebecca is a wonderful person. I don't think I've ever met a *(kind)* _____ and *(generous)* _____ person.

15. You can trust her. You will never meet a *(honest)* _____ person _____ she is.

16. I'm leaving! This is *(bad)* _____ movie I've ever seen! I won't sit through another second of it.

17. *(important)* _____ piece of equipment for birdwatching is a pair of binoculars.

18. Although both jobs are important, being a teacher requires *(education)* _____ _____ being a bus driver.

19. The Great Wall of China is the *(long)* _____ structure that has ever been built.

20. Howard Anderson is one of *(delightful)* _____ people I've ever met.

21. *(hard)* _____ I tried, *(impossible)* _____ it seemed to solve the math problem.

22. Perhaps *(common)* _____ topic of everyday conversation _____ the world is the weather.

23. No animals can travel (fast) _____ birds. Birds are (fast) _____

_____ animals _____ all.

24. Most birds have small eyes, but not ostriches. Indeed, the eye of an ostrich is (large)

_____ its brain.

25. (great) _____ variety of birds _____ a single area can be found in

the rain forests of Southeast Asia and India.

26. I feel (safe) _____ in a plane _____ I do in a car.

27. Jakarta is (large) _____ city _____ Indonesia.

◇ PRACTICE 30—GUIDED STUDY: Review of comparatives and superlatives.
(Charts 13-1 → 13-8)

Directions: Complete the sentences. Use any appropriate form of the words in parentheses and
add any other necessary words.

1. Sometimes I feel like all of my friends are (intelligent) ___***more intelligent than***___ I am, and

yet sometimes they tell me that they think I am (smart) _____***the smartest***_____ person

_____***in***_____ the class.

2. One of (popular) _____ holidays _____ Japan is New Year's.

3. A mouse is (small) _____ a rat.

4. Europe is first in agricultural production of potatoes. (potatoes) _____

are grown in Europe _____ on any other continent.

5. Mercury is (close) _____ planet to the sun. It moves around the sun (fast)

_____ any other plant in the solar system.

6. Human beings must compete with other species for the food of the land. The (great)

_____ competitors we have for food are insects.

7. When the temperature stays below freezing for a long period of time, the Eiffel Tower becomes

six inches (fifteen centimeters) (short) _____ .

8. Have you ever been bothered by a fly buzzing around you? (easy) _____

way _____ all to get a fly out of a room is to darken the room and turn on a light

somewhere else.

9. Mountain climbing takes (strength) _____ walking on a level path.

10. Cheese usually tastes (good) _____ at room temperature _____ it does

just after you take it out of the refrigerator.

11. World Cup Soccer is (big) _____ sporting event _____ the world. It

is viewed on TV by (people) _____ any other event in sports.

12. The wall of a soap bubble is very, very thin. A human hair is approximately ten thousand times

    (thick) _____ the wall of a soap bubble.

13. English has approximately 600,000 words. Because of the explosion of scientific discoveries

    and new technologies, there are *(words)* _____ in English _____

    in any other language.

14. You'd better buy the tickets for the show soon. *(long)* _____ you wait,

    (difficult) _____ it will be to get good seats.

15. I've seen a lot of funny movies over the years, but the one I saw last night is *(funny)*

    _____ all.

16. Riding a bicycle can be dangerous. *(people)* _____ were killed in

    bicycle accidents last year _____ have been killed in airplane accidents in the last four

    years.

17. Young people have *(high)* _____ rate of automobile accidents _____

    all drivers.

18. Some people build their own boats from parts that they order from a manufacturer. They save

    money that way. It is *(expensive)* _____ to build your own boat

    _____ to buy a boat.

19. It's easy to drown a houseplant. *(houseplants)* _____ die from too much water

    _____ not enough water.

20. Mr. Hochingnauong feels *(comfortable)* _____ speaking his native

language _____ he does speaking English.

21. My friend has studied many languages. He thinks Japanese is *(difficult)* _____

_____ all the languages he has studied.

22. One of *(bad)* _____ nuclear accidents _____ the world occurred at

Chernobyl in 1986.

23. I think learning a second language is *(hard)* _____ studying

chemistry or mathematics.

24. *(low)* _____ temperature ever recorded in Alaska was minus 80°F (-27° C) in

1971.

25. Computers are complicated machines, but one of *(complex)* _____

things _____ the universe is the human brain.

◇ PRACTICE 31—SELFSTUDY: *The same, similar, different, like, and alike.* (Chart 13-9)

Directions: Complete the sentences with AS, TO, FROM, or Ø if no word is necessary.

1. Geese are similar ____**to**____ ducks. They are both large water birds.

2. But geese are not the same ____**as**____ ducks. Geese are usually larger and have longer

necks.

3. Geese are different ____**from**____ ducks.

4. Geese are like ____**Ø**____ ducks in some ways, but geese and ducks are not exactly alike

____**Ø**____.

5. An orange is similar _____ a grapefruit. They are both citrus fruits.

6. But an orange is not the same _____ a grapefruit. A grapefruit is usually larger and

sourer.

7. An orange is different _____ a grapefruit.

8. An orange is like _____ a grapefruit in some ways, but they are not exactly alike

_____.

9. Gold is similar _____ silver. They are both valuable metals that people use for jewelry.

But they aren't the same _____. Gold is not the same color _____ silver. Gold

is also different _____ silver in cost. Gold is more expensive than silver.

10. Look at the two zebras. Their names are Zee and Bee. Zee looks like _____ Bee. Is Zee exactly the same _____ Bee? The pattern of the stripes on each zebra in the world is unique. No two zebras are exactly alike _____. Even though Zee and Bee are similar _____ each other, they are different _____ each other in the exact pattern of their stripes.

◇ PRACTICE 32—SELFSTUDY: *The same, similar, different, like,* and *alike.* (Chart 13-9)

Directions: Circle the correct completions.

1. My coat is   (*different,*) *the same*   from yours.

2. Our apartment is   *like, similar*   to my cousin's.

3. The news report on channel four was   *similar, the same*   as the report we heard on channel six last night.

4. My sister and I look   *like, alike*   and talk   *like, alike,*   but our personalities are quite   *different, similar to.*

5. Does James act   *like, alike*   his brother?

6. My dictionary is   *different, similar*   from yours.

7. A: I'm sorry, but I believe you have my umbrella.

   B: Oh? Yes, I see. It looks almost exactly   *like, alike*   mine, doesn't it?

8. A: How do you like the spaghetti I made for you? Is it   *similar, the same*   to yours?

   B: It's a little   *similar, like*   mine, but not exactly   *like, alike.*

9. A: Your jacket is exactly the same   *as, like*   mine.

   B: Isn't that amazing? I bought mine in New York, and you bought yours in Tokyo, and yet they're exactly   *the same, like.*

10. A: Some people think that we look   *like, alike.*   What do you think?

    B: Well, the color of your hair is   *similar, the same*   to mine, and your eyes are almost   *a similar, the same*   color as mine. I guess there's a resemblance.

◇ PRACTICE 33—GUIDED STUDY: *The same, similar, different, like,* and *alike.* (Chart 13-9)

Directions: Compare the figures. Complete the sentences using THE SAME, SIMILAR, DIFFERENT, LIKE, and ALIKE.

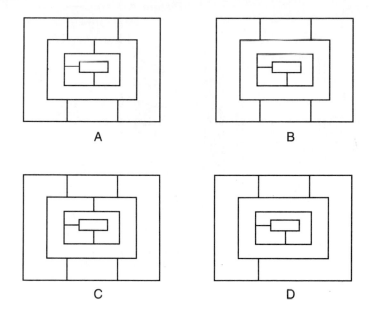

1. All of the figures are _____*similar to*_____ each other.

2. Figure A is _____ Figure B.

3. Figure A and Figure B are _____.

4. A and C are _____.

5. A and C are _____ D.

6. C is _____ A.

7. B isn't _____ D.

◇ PRACTICE 34—GUIDED STUDY: *The same, similar, different, like,* and *alike.* (Chart 13-9)

Directions: Compare the figures.

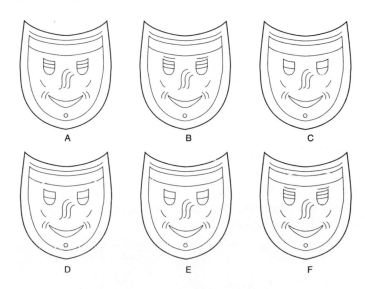

◇ PRACTICE 35—GUIDED STUDY: Making comparisons. (Chapter 13)

Directions: Compare the pictures. How many differences can you find?

Example: The boy in Picture B isn't the same height as the boy in Picture A .

◇ PRACTICE 36—GUIDED STUDY: Making comparisons. (Chapter 13)

Directions: Ask three (or more) classmates four (or more) questions.
First decide what you want to ask your classmates. Below are some suggestions.
Next fill out the chart with the topics of the questions.
Then write in the names of the classmates you talk to and ask them the questions.
After you have all of your information, compare the answers using SAME, DIFFERENT, SIMILAR, LIKE, ALIKE, AS . . . AS, MORE/-ER and MOST/-EST.

Example:

	eye-color	favorite sport	length of time at this school	educational goals	size of family
Hamid	brown	soccer	3 mo.	engineering degree	5
Hiroki	brown	baseball	3 mo.	business degree	4
Maria	brown	baseball	4 mo.	journalism degree	7

Possible comparisons:

I'm comparing three people: Hamid, Hiroki, and Maria.

• All three have **the same** eye color.

• Hiroki and Maria like **the same** sport, baseball. Hamid's favorite sport is **different from** theirs. He likes soccer.

- Maria has been at this school **longer than** Hamid and Hiroki.
- Their educational goals are **similar.** All of them want to get university degrees.
- Maria has **the largest** family. Hiroki's immediate family is **the smallest**.

Suggestions for questions to ask your classmates:

1. How long have you been at this school?
2. What color are your eyes?
3. What is your favorite kind of music?
4. What is your favorite sport?
5. What do you usually wear to class?
6. What are your educational goals?
7. How many people are there in your immediate family?*
8. How big is your hometown?
9. What kind of books do you like to read?
10. What kind of movies do you prefer?
11. What country would you most like to visit?
12. What is your favorite food?
13. When did you last visit home?
14. What kind of vacation do you prefer?
15. How tall are you?

Use this chart to record your information. Write in the topics of your questions, the names of the people you interview, and then their answers.

Immediate family = mother, father, and children (not including cousins, aunts, uncles, grandparents, etc.).

CHAPTER 14
Noun Clauses

◇ PRACTICE 1—SELFSTUDY: Noun clauses and information questions.
(Charts 6-2 and 14-2)

Directions: If the sentence contains a NOUN CLAUSE, underline it and circle NOUN CLAUSE. If the question word introduces a question, circle QUESTION. Add appropriate final punctuation: a PERIOD (.)* or a QUESTION MARK (?).

1. I don't know <u>where Jack bought his new boots</u>.   (NOUN CLAUSE)   QUESTION

2. Where did Jack buy his new boots?   NOUN CLAUSE   (QUESTION)

3. I don't understand why Ann left   NOUN CLAUSE   QUESTION

4. Why did Ann leave   NOUN CLAUSE   QUESTION

5. I don't know where your book is   NOUN CLAUSE   QUESTION

6. Where is your book   NOUN CLAUSE   QUESTION

7. When did Bob come   NOUN CLAUSE   QUESTION

8. I don't know when Bob came   NOUN CLAUSE   QUESTION

9. What does "calm" mean   NOUN CLAUSE   QUESTION

10. Tarik knows what "calm" means   NOUN CLAUSE   QUESTION

11. I don't know how long the earth has existed   NOUN CLAUSE   QUESTION

12. How long has the earth existed   NOUN CLAUSE   QUESTION

◇ PRACTICE 2—SELFSTUDY: Noun clauses and information questions.
(Charts 6-2 and 14-2)

Directions: PART I: Underline the NOUN CLAUSE in each sentence. Find the SUBJECT (**S**) and VERB (**V**) of the noun clause.

                                  S   **V**
1. I don't know <u>where [Patty] [went] last night</u>.

_____
*A *period* is called a *full stop* in British English.

2. Do you know where [Joe's parents] [live]?*

   S **V** (above "where [Joe's parents] [live]")

3. I know where   Joe   lives.

4. Do you know what time   the movie   begins?

5. She explained where   Brazil   is.

6. I don't believe what   Estefan   said.

7. I don't know when   the packages   will arrive.

8. Please tell me how far   it   is   to the post office.

9. I don't know   who   knocked   on the door.

10. I wonder   what   happened   at the party last night.

PART II: Change the <u>underlined</u> NOUN CLAUSE to a QUESTION.

1. QUESTION: **_Where did Patty go last night_** _____?

   NOUN CLAUSE: I don't know <u>where Patty went last night</u>.

2. QUESTION: **_Where do Joe's parents live_** _____?

   NOUN CLAUSE: I don't know <u>where Joe's parents live</u>.

3. QUESTION: _____?

   NOUN CLAUSE: I don't know <u>where Joe lives</u>.

4. QUESTION: _____?

   NOUN CLAUSE: I don't know <u>what time the movie begins</u>.

5. QUESTION: _____?

   NOUN CLAUSE: I don't know <u>where Pine Street is</u>.

6. QUESTION: _____?

   NOUN CLAUSE: I don't know <u>what Estefan said</u>.

7. QUESTION: _____?

   NOUN CLAUSE: I don't know <u>when the packages will arrive</u>.

8. QUESTION: _____?

   NOUN CLAUSE: I don't know <u>how far it is to the post office</u>.

---

*A question mark is used at the end of this noun clause because the main subject and verb of the sentence (*Do you know*) are in question word order.
  Example: *Do you know where Joe lives?*
Do you know asks a question; *where Joe lives* is a noun clause.

9. QUESTION: _____?

NOUN CLAUSE: I don't know <u>who knocked on the door</u>.

10. QUESTION: _____?

NOUN CLAUSE: I don't know <u>what happened at the party last night</u>.

◇ PRACTICE 3—SELFSTUDY: Noun clauses that begin with a question word. (Chart 14-2)

Directions: Complete the dialogues by changing the questions to NOUN CLAUSES.

1. A: Where does Jim go to school?

B: I don't know _____*where Jim goes*_____ to school.

2. A: Where did Alex go yesterday?

B: I don't know. Do you know _____*where Alex went*_____ yesterday?

3. A: Why is Maria laughing?

B: I don't know. Does anybody know _____?

4. A: Why is fire hot?

B: I don't know _____ hot.

5. A: How much does a new Honda cost?

B: Peter can tell you _____.

6. A: Why is Mike always late?

B: Don't ask me. I don't understand _____ late.

7. A: How long do birds live?

B: I don't know _____.

8. A: When was the first wheel invented?

B: I don't know. Do you know _____?

9. A: How many hours does a light bulb burn?

B: I don't know exactly _____.

10. A: Where did Emily buy her computer?

B: I don't know _____ her computer.

11. A: Who lives next door to Kate?

B: I don't know _____ next door to Kate.

12. A: Who(m) did Julie talk to?

B: I don't know _____ to.

◇ PRACTICE 4—SELFSTUDY: Noun clauses and information questions.
(Charts 6-2 and 14-2)

Directions: Complete the sentences with the words in parentheses.

1. A: Do you know where *(Jason, work)* _____ **Jason works** _____?

B: Who?

A: Jason. Where *(he, work)* _____ **does he work** _____?

B: I don't know.

2. A: Where *(Susan, eat)* _____ lunch yesterday?

B: I don't know where *(she, eat)* _____ lunch yesterday.

3. A: Excuse me.

B: Yes. How can I help you?

A: How much *(that camera, cost)* _____?

B: You want to know how much *(this camera, cost)* _____,

is that right?

A: No, not that one. The one next to it.

4. A: How far *(you, can run)* _____ without stopping?

B: I have no idea. I don't know how far *(I, can run)* _____

without stopping. I've never tried.

5. A: Where *(you, see)* _____ the ad for the computer sale last

week?

B: I don't remember where *(I, see)* _____ it. One of the local

papers, I think.

6. A: Could you please tell me where *(Mr. Gow's office, is)* _____?

B: I'm sorry. I didn't understand.

A: Where *(Mr. Gow's office, is)* _____ _____ ?

B: Ah. Down the hall on the right.

7. A: Ann was out late last night, wasn't she? What time *(she, get)* _____ in?

   B: Why do you want to know what time *(she, get)* _____ home?

   A: Just curious.

8. A: What time *(it, is)* _____?

   B: I don't know. I'll ask Sara. Sara, do you know what time *(it, is)* _____?

   C: Almost four-thirty.

9. A: What was your score on the test?

   B: I don't know yet.

   A: How soon *(you, know)* _____ ?

   B: I don't know how soon *(I, know)* _____. I won't know until the professor hands the exams back.

10. A: How often *(you, go)* _____ shopping every week?

    B: *(you, mean)* _____ grocery shopping?

    A: Yes.

    B: Why? I don't understand why *(you, want)* _____ to know how often *(I, go)* _____ shopping every week.

    A: My mother goes to the market every day. She thinks I'm lazy because I go shopping only once a week. I just wonder how often *(other people, go)* _____ shopping.

    B: I see. Well, once a week is enough for me.

11. A: *(who, invent)* _____ the first refrigerator?

    B: I don't know *(who, invent)* _____ it. Do you?

12. A: Whose car *(Toshi, borrow)* _____ yesterday?

    B: I don't know whose car *(Toshi, borrow)* _____.

13. A: When *(Rachel, plan)* _____ to return to class?

    B: No one knows when *(she, return)* _____ to class. She left the hospital two weeks ago.

    A: Why *(she, be)* _____ in the hospital?

    B: I haven't heard why *(she, be)* _____ in the hospital. I just know that she's living at home with her parents.

14. A: Where *(Tom, go)* _____ last night?

    B: I'm sorry. I didn't hear what *(you, say)* _____.

    A: I wanted to know where *(Tom, go)* _____ last night.

◇ PRACTICE 5—SELFSTUDY: Noun clauses with *who, what, whose + be.* (Chart 14-3)

Directions: Find the SUBJECT (**S**) and VERB (**V**) of the NOUN CLAUSE.

                    S   **V**

1. I don't know who [that man] [is].

               S   **V**

2. I don't know [who] [called].

3. I don't know   who   those people   are.

4. I don't know   who   that person   is.

5. I don't know   who   lives   next door to me.

6. I don't know   who   my teacher   will be   next semester.

7. I don't know   who   will teach   us next semester.

8. I don't know   what   a lizard   is.

9. I don't know   what   happened   in class yesterday.

10. I don't know   whose hat   this   is.

11. I don't know   whose hat   is   on the table.

◇ PRACTICE 6—SELFSTUDY: Noun clauses with *who, what, whose + be.* (Chart 14-3)

Directions: Add the word **IS** to each sentence in the correct place.

1. I don't know who _____ that woman ____*is*____.

2. I don't know who ____*is*____ on the phone _____.

3. I don't know what _____ a crow _____.

4. I don't know what _____ in that bag _____.

5. I don't know whose car _____ in the driveway _____.

6. I don't know whose car _____ that _____.

7. I don't know who _____ Bob's doctor _____.

8. I don't know who _____ in the doctor's office _____.

◇ PRACTICE 7—SELFSTUDY: Noun clauses with *who, what, whose + be.* (Chart 14-3)

Directions: Complete the dialogues by changing the QUESTIONS to NOUN CLAUSES.

1. A: Whose car is that?

   B: I don't know ____*whose car that is*_____.

2. A: Whose car is in front of Sam's house?

   B: I don't know ____*whose car is in front of Sam's house*_____.

3. A: Who has the scissors?

    B: Not me. I don't know _____.

4. A: Who are the best students?

    B: Ask the teacher _____.

5. A: What is a violin?

    B: I don't know _____.

    C: It's a musical instrument that has strings.

6. A: What causes earthquakes?

    B: You should ask your geology professor _____.

7. A: What kind of fruit is that?

    B: I can't tell you _____. I've never seen it before.

8. A: Whose hammer is this?

    B: I don't know. Hey, Hank, do you know _____?

    A: It's Ralph's.

9. A: The phone's for you.

    B: Who is it?

    A: I don't know _____. Want me to find out?

    B: Yeah.

    A: Okay.   Could I please ask who's calling? Oh, hi, Jennifer! It's Jennifer.

    B: Where is she?

    A: Betsy wants to know _____. Okay. She's at home.

    B: What time does she want me to meet her at the theater?

    A: Here. You talk to her yourself.

◇ PRACTICE 8—GUIDED STUDY: Noun clauses and information questions.
                            (Charts 6-2, 14-2 and 14-3)

   Directions: Complete the sentences with the words in parentheses.

   1. A: How long *(the oldest whales, live)* ___***do the oldest whales live***_____?

       B: Nobody knows for sure how long *(the oldest whales, live)* ___***the oldest whales live***___.

   2. A: Do you know how old *(Amanda, be)* _____?

       B: Why do you want to know how old *(Amanda, be)* _____?

       A: Just answer my question. How old *(Amanda, be)* _____?

       B: I won't tell you until you tell me why *(you, want)* _____ to

           know.

3. A: The boss wants to know why *(David, leave)* _____ the office

   early yesterday. Do you know?

   B: No. I'll ask Sara. Hey, Sara, why *(David, leave)* _____

   early yesterday?

   C: He had to go to a meeting at his son's school.

4. A: How *(airplanes, stay)* _____ up in the air?

   B: What? What are you talking about?

   A: I'm talking about airplanes. I wonder how *(they, stay)* _____

   up in the air. Do you know?

   B: Sure. It has something to do with the movement of air.

5. A: Where *(you, go)* _____ last night?

   B: I don't have to tell you where *(I, go)* _____ last night.

   A: Why don't you want to tell me where *(you, go)* _____ last night?

   B: It's none of your business.

   A: Well!

6. A: What *(an apricot, be)* _____ ?

   B: Why do you want to know what *(an apricot, be)* _____?

   A: I'm studying my vocabulary list. I'm trying to learn twenty new words every day.

   B: I see. An apricot is a small, sweet, orange fruit.

7. A: Do you know why *(Jane, bring)* _____

   her suitcase to work with her this morning?

   B: No. I'll ask Mike. Mike, why *(Jane, bring)* _____

   her suitcase to work with her this morning? Did she tell you?

   C: Yes. Right after work today she's leaving for Springfield to visit her fiancé.

8. A: Whose red sports car *(that, be)* _____ ?

   B: I'll ask Don. I think he knows whose red sports car *(that, be)* _____ .

   A: Wish it were mine.

9. A: What *("chief," mean)* _____ ?

   B: What's the word?

   A: "Chief." I want to know what *("chief," mean)* _____ ?

   B: I don't know. Pablo, do you know what *("chief," mean)* _____ ?

   C: No. I'll ask the teacher. Ms. Sills, what *("chief," mean)* _____ ,

   as in "the chief reason"?

   D: It means "Principal, main, most important."

10. A: Mom, why *(some people, be)* _____ cruel to other people?

    B: Honey, I don't really understand why *(some people, be)* _____

    cruel to others. It's difficult to explain.

11. A: Mr. Wortman! Why *(you, tell, not)* _____ me about

    this problem sooner?

    B: I'm sorry, sir. I don't know why *(I, tell, not)* _____

    you about it sooner. I guess I forgot.

12. A: What kind of camera *(Barbara, have)* _____ ?

    B: I don't know, but you should find out what kind of camera *(she, have)*

    _____ before you decide what to get for yourself. She knows a lot

    about cameras.

13. A: How many French francs *(there, be)* _____ in one U.S. dollar?

    B: I don't know. Call your friend Pierre if you want to know how many French francs *(there,

    be)* _____ in one U.S. dollar.

14. A: Susan looks sad. Why *(she, be)* _____ so unhappy today?

    B: I can't say why *(she, be)* _____ unhappy. She swore me to secrecy.

15. A: I don't care about the future. All I care about is today.

    B: Oh? Well, answer this question for me. Where *(you, spend)* _____

    _____ the rest of your life?

    A: What do you mean?

    B: I mean it's important to pay attention to the future. That's where *(you, spend)*

    _____ the rest of your life.

◇ PRACTICE 9—GUIDED STUDY: Information questions and noun clauses.
(Charts 6-2, 14-2, and 14-3)

Directions: Ask information questions and respond using NOUN CLAUSES.

STUDENT A: Using the given question word, ask a question that you are sure Student B cannot
answer. (You don't have to know the answer to the question.)
STUDENT B: Respond to the question by saying "I don't know . . ." followed by a NOUN CLAUSE.
Then you can guess at an answer if you wish.

Example: when
STUDENT A: *When was the first book printed?*
STUDENT B: *I don't know when the first book was printed. Probably three or four hundred years ago.*

1. where	6. whose
2. who	7. when
3. how far	8. why
4. what kind	9. what
5. what time	10. how much

◇ PRACTICE 10—SELFSTUDY: *Yes/no* questions and noun clauses. (Charts 6-2 and 14-4)

Directions: Change the YES/NO QUESTION to a NOUN CLAUSE.

1. YES/NO QUESTION: Is Tom coming?

   NOUN CLAUSE: I wonder _____ **if (whether) Tom is coming** _____.

2. YES/NO QUESTION: Can Jennifer play the piano?

   NOUN CLAUSE: I don't know _____.

3. YES/NO QUESTION: Did Paul go to work yesterday?

   NOUN CLAUSE: I don't know _____.

4. YES/NO QUESTION: Is Susan coming to work today?

   NOUN CLAUSE: Can you tell me _____?

5. YES/NO QUESTION: Will Mr. Pips be at the meeting?

   NOUN CLAUSE: Do you know _____?

6. YES/NO QUESTION: Is Barcelona a coastal town?

   NOUN CLAUSE: I can't remember _____.

7. YES/NO QUESTION: Would Carl like to come with us?

   NOUN CLAUSE: I wonder _____.

8. YES/NO QUESTION: Do you still have Yung Soo's address?

   NOUN CLAUSE: I don't know _____.

Directions: Complete the dialogues by completing the NOUN CLAUSES. Use **IF** to introduce the noun clause.

1. A: Are you tired?

    B: Why do you want to know _____*if I am*_____ tired?

    A: You look tired. I'm worried about you.

2. A: Are you going to be in your office later today?

    B: What? Sorry. I didn't hear you.

    A: I need to know _____ in your office later today.

3. A: Do all birds have feathers?

    B: Well, I don't really know for sure _____ feathers,

    but I suppose they do.

4. A: Did Bill take my dictionary off my desk?

    B: Who?

    A: Bill. I want to know _____ my dictionary off my desk.

5. A: Can Uncle Pete babysit tonight?

    B: Sorry. I wasn't listening. I was thinking about something else.

    A: Have you talked to Uncle Pete? We need to know _____ tonight.

6. A: Does Al have a flashlight in his car?

    B: I'll ask him. Hey, Al! Al! Fred wants to know _____

    a flashlight in your car.

7. A: Are you going to need help moving the furniture to your new apartment?

    B: I don't know _____ help. Thanks for asking. I'll

    let you know.

8. A: Should I take my umbrella?

    B: How am I supposed to know _____ your umbrella? I'm

    not a weather forecaster.

    A: You're kind of grumpy today, aren't you?

9. A: Is white a color?

    B: What?

    A: I wonder _____ a color, you know, like blue or red.

    B: Of course it is.

10. A: Can fish smell?

   B: Why do you want to know _____ ?

   A: Just wondering. Do fish breathe?

   B: You want to know _____ , is that right?

   A: Yes. Do they?

   B: Sort of. They get oxygen from water through their gills.

◇ PRACTICE 12—GUIDED STUDY: Noun clauses. (Charts 14-1 → 14-4)

Directions: What are some of the things you wonder about? Consider the given topics. Create sentences with "**I wonder . . . (why, when, how, if, whether, etc.).**"

1. birds → *I wonder how many birds there are in the world.*
   I wonder how many different kinds of birds there are in the world.
   I wonder how long birds have lived on earth.
   I wonder whether birds can communicate with each other.
   I wonder if birds in cages are unhappy.

2. fish

3. the earth

4. (*name of a person you know*)

5. events in the future

6. electricity

7. dinosaurs

8. (*topic of your own choosing*)

◇ PRACTICE 13—GUIDED STUDY: Questions and noun clauses.
                      (Charts 6-2 and 14-1 → 14-4)

Directions: Make up questions and report them using NOUN CLAUSES.

STUDENT A: Write five questions you want to ask Student B about his/her life or opinions. Sign your name. Hand the questions to Student B.

STUDENT B: Report to the class or a smaller group what Student A wants to know and then provide the information if you can or want to. Use " . . . wants to know . . ." each time you report a question.

Example:

STUDENT A's list of questions:

1. Where were you born?

2. What is your favorite color?

3. What do you think about the recent election in your country?

4. Who do you admire most in the world?

5. Do you have a red car?

STUDENT B's report:

1. (Student A) wants to know where I was born. I was born in (Caracas).

2. S/he wants to know what my favorite color is. Well, blue, I guess.

3. S/he wants to know what I think about the recent election in my country. I'm very pleased. The new leader will be good for my country.

4. (S/he) wants to know who I admire most in the world. I'll have to think about that for a minute.

5. Finally, (s/he) wants to know if I have a red car. I wonder why s/he wants to know that. The answer is no. I don't have a red car, or a black car, or a blue car.

◇ PRACTICE 14—GUIDED STUDY: Questions and noun clauses. (Charts 6-2, 14-1 → 14-4)

Directions: Make up questions and answer them using NOUN CLAUSES.

STUDENT A: Ask a question. Use the suggestions below.
STUDENT B: Answer the question if you can. If you can't, respond by saying "I don't know . . ." followed by a NOUN CLAUSE. Then you can guess at the answer if you wish.

Example: location of X★
STUDENT A: *Where is Mr. Chin's briefcase right now?*
STUDENT B: *Under his desk.*   OR
            I don't know where his briefcase is right now. I suppose he left it at home today.

1. location of X
2. cost of X
3. year that X happened
4. reason for X
5. person who did X
6. owner of X
7. the meaning of X
8. time of X
9. amount of X
10. country X is from
11. type of X
12. distance from X to Y

◇ PRACTICE 15—SELFSTUDY: *That*-clauses. (Chart 14-5)

Directions: Add the word THAT to the following sentences at the appropriate places to mark the beginning of a noun clause.

1. I believe ∧ **that** we need to protect endangered species of animals.

2. Last night I dreamed I was at my aunt's house.

3. I think most people have kind hearts.

4. I know Matt walks a long distance to school every day. I assume he doesn't have a bicycle.

5. I heard Sara dropped out of school.

6. Did you notice Ji Ming wasn't in class yesterday? I hope he's okay.

★"X" simply indicates that the questioner should supply her/his own ideas.

7. I trust Linda. I believe what she said. I believe she told the truth.

8. A: Can Julia prove her watch was stolen?

   B: I suppose she can't, but she suspects her roommate's friend took it.

9. A: Did you know leopards sometimes keep their dead prey in trees?

   B: Really?

   A: Yes. I understand they save their food for later if they're not hungry.

10. A: Do you believe a monster really exists in Loch Ness in Scotland?

    B: I don't know. Look at this story in the newspaper. It says some scientists have proved the Loch Ness Monster exists.

    A: You shouldn't always believe what you read in the newspapers. I think the monster is purely fictional.

◇ PRACTICE 16—SELFSTUDY: *That*-clauses. (Charts 14-5 and 14-7)

Directions: Add the word **THAT** to the following sentences at the appropriate places to mark the beginning of a noun clause.

      that
1. I'm sorry ∧ you won't be here for Joe's party.

2. I'm glad it's warm today.

3. I'm surprised you bought a car.

4. Are you certain Mr. McVay won't be here tomorrow?

5. John is pleased Claudio will be here for the meeting.

6. Carmella was convinced I was angry with her, but I wasn't.

7. Jason was angry his father wouldn't let him use the family car.

8. Andy was fortunate you could help him with his algebra. He was delighted he got a good grade on the exam.

9. It's a fact the Nile River flows north.

10. It's true some dinosaurs could fly.

11. Are you aware dinosaurs lived on earth for one hundred and twenty-five million (125,000,000) years?

12. Is it true human beings have lived on earth for only four million (4,000,000) years?

◇ PRACTICE 17—GUIDED STUDY: *That*-clauses. (Charts 14-5 and 14-7)

Directions: Add the word **THAT** to the following sentences at the appropriate places to mark the beginning of a noun clause.

1. A: Are you sure ∧*that* you'll be in class tomorrow?

   B: Yes. I'm certain ∧*that* I'll be in class tomorrow. It's a test day.

2. A: Guido is delighted you can speak Italian.

   B: I'm surprised he can understand my Italian. It's not very good.

3. A: How do you know it's going to be nice tomorrow?

   B: I heard the weather report.

   A: So? The weather report is often wrong, you know. I'm still worried it'll rain on our picnic.

4. A: Are you afraid another diasaster like the one at Chernobyl might occur?

   B: Yes. I'm convinced it can happen again.

5. A: Are you aware you have to pass the English test to get into the university?

   B: Yes, but I'm not worried about it. I'm positive I'll do well on it.

6. A: Mrs. Lane hopes we can come with her to the museum tomorrow.

   B: I don't think I can go with you. I'm supposed to babysit my little brother tomorrow.

   A: Oh, too bad. I wish you could come.

7. A: Is it a fact blue whales are the largest creatures on earth?

   B: Yes. In fact, I believe they are the largest creatures that have ever lived on earth.

8. A: Do you think technology benefits humankind?

B: Of course. Everyone knows modern inventions make our lives better.

A: I'm not sure that's true. For example, cars and buses provide faster transportation, but they pollute our air. Air pollution can cause lung disease and other illnesses.

◇ PRACTICE 18—GUIDED STUDY: *That*-clauses. (Charts 14-5 and 14-7)

Directions: Read each dialogue. Then use the expressions in parentheses to explain what the people are talking about.

DIALOGUE 1. ALICIA: I really like my English teacher.
BONNIE: Great! That's wonderful. It's important to have a good English teacher.
             (think that, be delighted that)
→ *Alicia thinks that her English teacher is very good.*
   Bonnie is delighted that Alicia likes her English teacher.
   Alicia is delighted that she has a good English teacher.
   Bonnie thinks that it's important to have a good English teacher.

DIALOGUE 2. MR. GREEN: Why didn't you return my call?
MS. WHITE: I truly apologize. I just got too busy and it slipped my mind.
             (be upset that, be sorry that,)
→ *Mr. Green is upset that Ms. White didn't return his call.*
   Ms. White is upset that she forgot to call Mr. Green.
   Ms. White is sorry that she didn't call Mr. Green.

DIALOGUE 3. MRS. DAY: How do you feel, honey? You might have the flu.
BOBBY: I'm okay, Mom. Honest. I don't have the flu.
             (be worried that, be sure that)

DIALOGUE 4. KIM: Did you really fail your chemistry course? How is that possible?
TINA: I didn't study hard enough. I was too busy having fun with my friends. I feel terrible about it.
             (be surprised that, be disappointed that)

DIALOGUE 5. KAY: Oh no! My dog is lost! My poor little dog!
            SARA: Call your neighbor. Your dog is probably visiting your neighbor's dog.
                   (be afraid that, think that)

DIALOGUE 6. DAVID: Mike! Hello! It's nice to see you.
            MIKE: It's nice to be here. Thank you for inviting me.
                   (be glad/happy/pleased that)

DIALOGUE 7. FRED: Susan has left. Look. Her closet is empty. Her suitcases are gone. She
                   won't be back. I just know it!
            ERICA: She'll be back.
                   (be afraid that, be upset that, be sure that)

DIALOGUE 8. JOHN: I heard you were in jail. I couldn't believe it!
            ED: Neither could I! I was arrested for robbing a house on my block. Can you
                   believe that? It was a case of mistaken identity. I didn't have to stay in jail
                   long.
                   (be shocked that, be relieved that)

◇ PRACTICE 19—GUIDED STUDY: *That*-clauses. (Charts 14-5 and 14-7)

Directions: What are your views on the following topics? Introduce your opinion with an
expression in the given list, then state your opinion in a **THAT**-CLAUSE.

am certain that	*believe that*	*hope that*
am convinced that	*can prove that*	*predict that*
am sure that	*have concluded that*	*think that*

Example: guns
→ *I believe that ordinary people shouldn't have guns in their homes.*
   I think anyone should be able to have any kind of gun.
   I have concluded that countries in which it is easy to get a gun have a higher
   rate of murder than other countries do.

1. smoking (cigarettes, cigars, pipes)
2. a controversy at your school (perhaps something that has been on the front pages of a student newspaper)
3. a recent political event in the world (something that has been on the front pages of the newspapers)
4. the exploration of outer space
5. the older generation vs. the younger generation
6. strong laws to protect the environment and endangered species
7. freedom of the press vs. government controlled news
8. solutions to world hunger

◇ PRACTICE 20—SELFSTUDY: Substituting *so* for a *that*-clause. (Chart 14-6)

Directions: Give the meaning of **SO** by writing a **THAT**-clause.

1. A: Does Alice have a car?
   B: I don't think so. (= *I don't think* _____**that Alice has a car**_____ .)

2. A: Did Alex pass his French course?

   B: I think so. (= *I think* _____.)

3. A: Is Mr. Kozari going to be at the meeting?

   B: I hope so. (= *I hope* _____.)

4. A: Can cats swim?

   B: I think so. (= *I think* _____.)

5. A: Do gorillas have tails?

   B: I don't think so. (= *I don't think* _____.)

6. A: Will Janet be at Omar's wedding?

   B: I suppose so. (= *I suppose* _____.)

◇ PRACTICE 21—GUIDED STUDY: Substituting *so* for a *that*-clause. (Chart 14-6)

Directions: Working with another student, complete the dialogues with your own words.

STUDENT A: Complete the question.
STUDENT B: Complete the response using **THINK, BELIEVE, HOPE,** or **SUPPOSE.**

1. A: Does Maria have _____*any brothers or sisters*_____?

   B: I _____*don't think*_____ so.

2. A: Do you know if _____*Mr. Miranda will be in class*_____ tomorrow?

   B: I _____*hope*_____ so .

3. A: Is Singapore farther north than _____?

   B: I _____ so.

4. A: Will peace be a reality soon in _____?

   B: I _____ so.

5. A: Can most adults _____?

   B: I _____ so.

6. A: Do you have _____ in your _____?

   B: I _____ so.

7. A: Is _____ soon?

   B: I _____ so.

8. A: Will our teacher _____?

   B: I _____ so.

9. A: Is _____ a holiday in India?

   B: I _____ so.

10. A: Was _____?

    B: I _____ so.

CHAPTER 15
Quoted Speech and Reported Speech

◇ PRACTICE 1—SELFSTUDY: Quoted speech. (Chart 15-1)

> Directions: All of the following present quoted speech. Punctuate as necessary by adding QUOTATION MARKS ("..."),* COMMAS (,), PERIODS (.),** and QUESTION MARKS (?). Also use capital letters as necessary.

> *Example:* My roommate said the door is open could you close it
>
> → My roommate said, "The door is open. Could you close it?"

1. Alex said do you smell smoke

2. He said something is burning

3. He said do you smell smoke something is burning

4. Rachel said the game starts at seven

5. She said the game starts at seven we should leave here at six

6. She said the game starts at seven we should leave here at six can you be ready to leave then

---
* Quotation marks are called *inverted commas* in British English.
** A *period* is called a *full stop* in British English.

◇ PRACTICE 2—SELFSTUDY: Quoted speech. (Chart 15-1)

(a) "Cats are fun to watch**,**" Jane said.	In (a): Notice that a comma (not a period) is used at the end of the quoted **sentence** when *Jane said* comes after the quote.
(b) "Do you own a cat**?**" Mike said.	In (b): Notice that a question mark (not a comma) is used at the end of the quoted **question**.

Directions: Notice the punctuation in examples (a) and (b) above. All of the following present quoted speech. Punctuate as necessary by adding QUOTATION MARKS ("**. . .**"), COMMAS (**,**), PERIODS (**.**), and QUESTION MARKS (**?**). Also use CAPITAL LETTERS as necessary.

Example: The door is open my roommate said.

→ *"**T**he door is open**,**" my roommate said.*

Example: The door is open could you close it my roommate said

→ *"**T**he door is open**.** **C**ould you close it**?**" my roommate said.*

1. Do you smell smoke   Alex said

2. Something is burning   he said

3. Do you smell smoke   something is burning   he said

4. The game starts at seven   Rachel said

5. The game starts at seven   we should leave here at six   she said

6. Can you be ready to leave at six   she asked

7. The game starts at seven   we should leave here at six   can you be ready to leave then she said

8. The game starts at seven   she said   we should leave here at six   can you be ready to leave then

◇ PRACTICE 3—SELFSTUDY: Quoted speech. (Chart 15-1)

Directions: All of the following present quoted speech. Punctuate by adding QUOTATION MARKS ("**. . .**"), COMMAS (**,**), PERIODS (**.**), and QUESTION MARKS (**?**) wherever needed. Also use CAPITAL LETTERS as necessary.

Example: Jack said please wait for me

→ Jack said**,** *"**P**please wait for me**.**"*

1. Mrs. Hill said my children used to take the bus to school

2. She said we moved closer to the school

3. Now my children can walk to school Mrs. Hill said

4. Do you live near the school she asked

5. Yes, we live two blocks away I replied

6. How long have you lived here Mrs. Hill wanted to know.

7. I said we've lived here for five years how long have you lived here

8. We've lived here for two years Mrs. Hill said how do you like living here

9. It's a nice community I said it's a good place to raise children

◇ PRACTICE 4—SELFSTUDY: Quoted speech. (Chart 15-1)

Directions: Following are two passages which use quoted speech. Punctuate as necessary by adding QUOTATION MARKS (" . . . "), COMMAS (,), PERIODS (.), QUESTION MARKS (?), and EXCLAMATION MARKS (!). Notice that a new paragraph begins each time the speaker changes.

CONVERSATION 1:

"Why weren't you in class yesterday?" Mr. Garcia asked me.

I had to stay home and take care of my pet bird I said. He wasn't feeling well.

What? Did you miss class because of your pet bird Mr. Garcia demanded to know.

I replied yes, sir. That's correct. I couldn't leave him alone. He looked so miserable.

Now I've heard every excuse in the world Mr. Garcia said. Then he threw his arms in the air and walked away.

CONVERSATION 2:

Both of your parents are deaf, aren't they I asked Robert.

Yes, they are he replied.

I'm looking for someone who knows sign language I said. Do you know sign language I asked.

Of course I do. I've been using sign language with my parents since I was a baby he said. It's a beautiful and expressive language. I often prefer it to spoken language.

Well, a deaf student is going to visit our class next Monday. Could you interpret for her I asked.

That's great he answered immediately and enthusiastically. I'd be delighted to. I'm looking forward to meeting her. Can you tell me why she is coming?

She's interested in seeing what we do in our English classes I said.

◇ PRACTICE 5—GUIDED STUDY: Quoted speech. (Chart 15-1)

Directions: Following are two passages that use quoted speech. Punctuate by adding QUOTATION MARKS (" . . .") and COMMAS (,) as necessary. Notice that a new paragraph begins each time the speaker changes.

One day my friend Laura and I were sitting in her apartment. We were having a cup of tea together and talking about the terrible earthquake that had just occurred in Iran. Laura asked me, "Have you ever been in an earthquake?"

Yes, I have I replied.

Was it a big earthquake she asked.

I've been in several earthquakes, and they've all been small ones I answered. Have you ever been in an earthquake?

There was an earthquake in my village five years ago Laura said. I was in my house. Suddenly the ground started shaking. I grabbed my little brother and ran outside. Everything was moving. I was scared to death. And then suddenly it was over.

I'm glad you and your brother weren't hurt I said.

Yes, we were very lucky.   Has everyone in the world felt an earthquake sometime in their lives Laura wondered. Do earthquakes occur everywhere on the earth?

Those are interesting questions I said but I don't know the answers.

◇ PRACTICE 6—GUIDED STUDY: Quoted speech. (Chart 15-1)

Directions: Rewrite the following. Punctuate as necessary by adding QUOTATION MARKS
(" . . ."") and COMMAS (,). Begin a new paragraph each time the speaker changes.

How did you do on the test my friend asked me. I replied I don't know yet. I won't know until
tomorrow. He said I know that it's an important test. Are you worried about your score? No, not
really I answered. I feel good about it. I think I did well on the test. That's great! he said. I like
people who have self-confidence.

◇ PRACTICE 7—SELFSTUDY: Reported speech: pronoun usage. (Charts 15-2 and 15-3)

Directions: Change the pronouns from quoted speech to REPORTED SPEECH.

1. QUOTED: Mr. Smith said, "I need help with my luggage."

   REPORTED: Mr. Smith said (that) _____ *he* _____ needed help with _____ *his* _____ luggage.

2. My roommate said to me, "You should call your brother."

   → My roommate said (that) _____ *I* _____ should call _____ *my* _____ brother.

3. Sarah said, "I like sugar in my coffee."

   → Sarah said (that) _____ liked sugar in _____ coffee.

4. Joe said to me, "I will call you."

   → Joe said (that) _____ would call _____.

5. My aunt said to me, "I want your new telephone number."

   → My aunt said (that) _____ wanted _____ new telephone number.

6. Sue and Tom said, "We don't like our new apartment."

   → Sue and Tom said (that) _____ didn't like _____ new apartment .

7. Sam said to me, "I've lost my book."

   → Sam said (that) _____ had lost _____ book.

8. Paul said to me, "I want you to help me with my homework."

   → Paul said (that) _____ wanted _____ to help _____ with

   _____ homework.

◇ PRACTICE 8—SELFSTUDY: Reported speech: sequence of tenses.
                          (Charts 15-2 and 15-3)

Directions: Complete the reported speech sentences. Use the formal sequence of tenses.

1. QUOTED: Sara said, "I need some help."

   REPORTED: Sara said (that) she _____ *needed* _____ some help.

2. Tom said, "I'm meeting David for dinner."

   → Tom said (that) he _____**was meeting**_____ David for dinner.

3. Ms. Davis said, "I have studied in Cairo."

   → Ms. Davis said (that) she _____ in Cairo.

4. Bill said, "I forgot to pay my electric bill."

   → Bill said (that) he _____ to pay his electric bill.

5. Barbara said, "I am exhausted."

   → Barbara said (that) she _____ exhausted.

6. I said, "I'll carry the box up the stairs."

   → I said (that) I _____ the box up the stairs.

7. Jerry said to me, "I can teach you to drive."

   → Jerry said (that) he _____ me to drive.

8. My sister said, "I have to attend a conference in London."

   → My sister said (that) she _____ a conference in London.

9. George said, "I should leave on Friday."

   → George said (that) he _____ on Friday.

10. Ed said, "I want a CD player."

    → Ed said (that) he _____ a CD player.

◇ PRACTICE 9—GUIDED STUDY: Reported speech: pronoun usage and sequence of tenses. (Charts 15-2 and 15-3)

Directions: Complete the reported speech sentences. Use the formal sequence of tenses.

1. QUOTED: David said to me, "I'm going to call you on Friday."

   REPORTED: David said (that) _____**he was going**_____

   _____**to call me**_____on Friday.

2. John said to Ann, "I have to talk to you."

   → John told Ann _____

   _____ to _____.

3. Diane said to me, "I can meet you after work."

   → Diane said _____

   _____ after work.

I HAVE TO
TALK TO YOU.

4. Maria said to Bob, "I wrote you a note."

→ Maria told Bob _____

_____ a note.

5. I said to David, "I need your help to prepare for the exam."

→ I told David _____

_____ help to prepare for the exam.

6. David said, "You should study with me."

→ David said _____

_____ with _____.

7. Julie asked Mike, "When will I see you again?"

→ Julie asked Mike when _____

_____ again.

8. Hillary said to Bill, "What are you doing?"

→ Hillary asked Bill _____

_____.

9. Mr. Fox said to me, "I'm going to meet Jack and you at the restaurant."

→ Mr. Fox said_____

_____ Jack and _____ at the restaurant.

10. A strange man looked at me and said, "I'm sure I've met you before."

→ A strange man looked at me and said _____ before. I was sure I'd never seen this person before in my whole life.

◇ PRACTICE 10—SELFSTUDY: *Say* vs. *tell.* (Chart 15-4)

Directions: Complete the sentences with **SAID** or **TOLD**.

1. Ann _____*told*_____ me that she was hungry.

2. Ann _____*said*_____ that she was hungry.

3. Jack _____ that I had a message.

4. Jack _____ me that I had a message.

5. My neighbor and I had a disagreement. I _____ my neighbor that he was wrong.

6. My neighbor _____ me that I was wrong.

7. Fumiko _____ the teacher that Fatima wasn't

   going to be in class.

8. Ellen _____ she enjoyed the movie last night.

9. When the storm began, I _____ the children

   to come into the house.

10. When I talked to Mr. Grant, he _____ he

    would be at the meeting.

◇ PRACTICE 11—SELFSTUDY: Reporting questions. (Chart 15-5)

Directions: Change the quoted questions to REPORTED QUESTIONS. Use formal sequence of tenses.

1. QUOTED: Eric said to me, "How old are you?"

   REPORTED: Eric asked me ___*how old I was*___.

2. Ms. Rush said to Mr. Long, "Are you going to be at the meeting?"

   → Ms. Rush asked Mr. Long ___*if he was going to be*___ at the meeting.

3. My mother said to me, "Can you hear the radio?"

   → My mother asked me _____ the radio.

4. I said to Abdullah, "Have you ever seen a panda?"

   → I asked Abdullah _____ a panda.

5. Mr. Lee said to his daughter, "Are you passing your biology class?"

   → Mr. Lee asked his daughter _____ _____ biology class.

6. Larry said to Ms. Ho, "Do you have time to help me?"

   → Larry asked Ms. Ho _____ time to help him.

7. Janet said to Bill, "When will you get back from your holiday?"

   → Janet asked Bill _____ _____ holiday.

8. Don said to Robert, "Did you change your mind about going to Reed College?"

   → Don asked Robert _____ mind about going to Reed College.

◇ PRACTICE 12—GUIDED STUDY: Reporting questions. (Chart 15-5)

Directions: Change the quoted questions to REPORTED QUESTIONS. Use **ASKED (SOMEONE)** to report the question. Use the formal sequence of tenses.

1. Igor said to me, "How long have you been a teacher?"

   → *Igor asked me how long I had been a teacher.*

2. Kathy said to Mr. May, "Will you be in your office around three?"
   → *Kathy asked Mr. May if he would be in his office around three.*

3. My brother said to me, "When do you plan to go to Bangkok?"

4. The teacher said to Maria, "Why are you laughing?"

5. My uncle said to me, "Have you ever considered a career in business?"

6. My boss said to me, "Did you bring the report with you?"

7. I said to Tina, "Can you speak Swahili?"

8. Bill said to Ann, "Are you tired?"

◇ PRACTICE 13—GUIDED STUDY: Reported vs. quoted speech. (Charts 15-2 → 15-5)

Directions: Change the reported speech to QUOTED SPEECH. Begin a new paragraph each time the speaker changes. Pay special attention to PRONOUNS, VERB FORMS, and WORD ORDER.

Example: This morning my mother asked me if I had gotten enough sleep last night. I told her that I was fine. I explained that I didn't need a lot of sleep. She told me that I needed to take better care of myself.

Written: *This morning my mother said, "Did you get enough sleep last night?"*
"I'm fine," I replied. "I don't need a lot of sleep."
She said, "You need to take better care of yourself."

1. In the middle of class yesterday, my friend tapped me on the shoulder and asked me what time it was. I told her it was two-thirty.

2. I met Mr. Redford at the reception for international students. He asked me where I was from. I told him I was from Argentina.

3. When I was putting on my hat and coat, Robert asked me where I was going. I told him that I had a date with Anna. He wanted to know what we were going to do. I told him that we were going to a movie.

◇ PRACTICE 14—GUIDED STUDY: Reported speech. (Charts 15-1 → 15-5)

Directions: Change the quoted speech to REPORTED SPEECH. Use formal sequence of tenses. In addition to using **SAID**, use verbs such as **TOLD, ASKED, WONDERED, WANTED TO KNOW, ANSWERED, REPLIED.**

Example:
QUOTED: "Where's Bill?" Susan asked me.
   "He's in the lunch room," I replied.
   "When will he be back in his office?" she wanted to know.
   I said, "He'll be back around two."
REPORTED: *Susan asked me where Bill was. I replied (that) he was in the lunch room. She wanted to know when he would be back in his office. I said (that) he would be back around two.*

1. "What are you doing?" Mr. Singh asked me.
   "I'm doing a grammar exercise," I told him.

2. "Where's my cane?" Grandfather asked me.
   "I don't know," I told him. "Do you need it?" I asked.
   "I want to walk to the mailbox," he said.
   I told him, "I'll find it for you."

3. "Can you help me clean the hall closet?" my wife asked me.
   "I'm really busy," I told her.
   "What are you doing?" she wanted to know.
   "I'm fixing the zipper on my winter jacket," I said.
   Then she asked me, "Will you have some time to help me after you fix the zipper?"
   I said, "I can't because I have to change a light bulb in the kitchen."
   With a note of exasperation in her voice, she finally said, "I'll clean the closet myself."

◇ PRACTICE 15—SELFSTUDY: Verb + infinitive to report speech. (Chart 15-6)

Directions: Change the quoted speech to reported speech by using a REPORTING VERB from the given list and an INFINITIVE. Use each verb from the list only one time.

advise	invite	remind
✔ask	order	warn
encourage	permit	

1. My son said, "Could you help me with my homework after dinner?"

   → My son _____*asked*_____ me _____*to help*_____ him with his

   homework after dinner.

2. Jennifer said to Kate, "Would you like to have dinner with me?"

   → Jennifer _____ Kate _____ dinner with her.

3. Mr. Crane said to his daughter, "You should take music lessons. You already sing very well. You would enjoy studying music. Wouldn't like you to learn how to play the piano?"

   → Mr Crane _____ his daughter _____ music

   lessons.

4. Nicole said to Heidi, "You should call Julie and apologize. At least, that's what I think."

   → Nicole _____ Heidi _____ Julie and

   _____.

5. Professor Wilson said to Bill, "Yes, you may use my name as a reference on your job application."

   → Professor Wilson _____ Bill _____ her name as

   a reference.

6. Robert said to his dog, "Sit."

   → Robert _____ his dog _____.

7. Kate said, "Don't forget to order some more large envelopes."

   → Kate _____ her secretary _____ some more

   large envelopes.

8. Mrs. Silverman said to her son, "Don't go near the water! I'm warning you! It's dangerous!"

   → Mrs. Silverman _____ her son _____ near the

   water.

◇ PRACTICE 16—GUIDED STUDY: Verb + infinitive to report speech. (Chart 15-6)

Directions: Change the quoted speech to reported speech by using a REPORTING VERB from the given list and completing the sentence.

    ✔ *advise*   *order*   *remind*
       encourage   *permit*   *warn*

1. I said to my daughter, "You should quit your job if you are unhappy."

   → I ____***advised my daughter to quit her job if she was unhappy***____.

2. The rebel commander said to his army, "Retreat!"

   → The rebel commander _____.

3. My aunt and uncle said to my husband and me, "Why don't you spend a week with us in August?"

   → My aunt and uncle _____.

4. Mr. Gordon said to his teenaged son, "Don't forget to make your bed."

   → Mr. Gordon _____.

5. The tour guide said to us, "Watch out for pickpockets in the marketplace."

   → The tour guide _____.

6. The teacher said to the students, "You may not leave the room in the middle of the examination."

   → The teacher didn't _____.

◇ PRACTICE 17—GUIDED STUDY: Verb + infinitive to report speech. (Chart 15-6)

Directions: Change the reported speech to QUOTED SPEECH. There is more than one possible completion. Use quotation marks and other punctuation as necessary.

1. Alex warned his friend not to drive faster than the speed limit.
   → Alex said to his friend . . . .
   Alex said to his friend, *"Don't drive faster than the speed limit."*
   Alex said to his friend, *"You'd better not drive faster than the speed limit."*

2. Paul had tickets to a soccer game. He invited Erica to go with him.
   → Paul said to Erica . . . .
   Paul said to Erica, *"Would you like to go to a soccer game with me?"*
   Paul said to Erica, *"Can you go to a soccer game with me?"*

3. Dr. Aqua advised his patient to drink eight glasses of water a day.

   → Dr. Aqua said to his patient . . . .

4. Mr. Nottingham allowed the children to go to the two o'clock movie at the mall.

   → Mr. Nottingham said to the children . . . .

5. Richard's school counselor encouraged him to enroll in a technical school.

   → Richard's school counselor said to him . . . .

6. The swimming instructor warned her beginning class not to go into the deep end of the pool.

   → The swimming instructor said to her beginning class . . . .

7. Debbie's mother reminded her not to forget her music lesson after school.

   → Debbie's mother said . . . .

8. Sue asked her neighbor Ann to look after the baby for a little while.

   → Sue said to her neighbor . . . .

9. Bill told us to wait for him at the corner of 6th and Pine.

   → Bill said to us . . . .

10. The CEO* ordered his staff to give him their financial reports by five o'clock.

    → The CEO said to his staff . . . .

◇ PRACTICE 18—GUIDED STUDY: Verb + infinitive to report speech. (Chart 15-6)

Directions: Use Student A's original ideas to report speech using a verb and infinitive.

STUDENT A: Speak to Student B, following the directions given in each item below.
STUDENT B: Report what Student A said to you using the *italicized* verb.

Example: advise Student B to do something
STUDENT A (Masako): *Maria, I think you should use an English–English dictionary instead of a Spanish–English dictionary.*
STUDENT B (Maria): *Masako advised me to use an English–English dictionary instead of a Spanish–English dictionary.*

1. *ask* Student B to do something
2. *remind* Student B to do something
3. *warn* Student B not to do something
4. *invite* Student B to do something
5. *advise* Student B to do (or not to do) something
6. *allow* Student B to do something
7. *encourage* Student B to do something
8. *tell* Student B to do (or not to do) something

◇ PRACTICE 19—GUIDED STUDY: Reporting speech. (Chapter 15)

Directions: Use your imagination. Who are these people and what are they saying?

STUDENT A: Give names to the people in the cartoons. Write what you imagine the people are saying in the empty cartoon balloons.
STUDENT B: Read what Student A wrote in the cartoon balloons. Write a story about the people in the cartoons. Write about who said what to whom.

Example: For Story 1, STUDENT A could name the people Mrs. Lee and Mr. Lee, and then write in the balloons:
Mrs. Lee: *Dinner's ready.*   Mr. Lee: *Okay. I'll be there in a minute.*
Mrs. Lee: *It's getting cold.*   Mr. Lee: *I have to hear the end of this news report.*

---

*CEO = an abbreviation for **C**hief **E**xecutive **O**fficer, meaning the head of a company or corporation.

Example of STUDENT B's written story, using **present tense reporting verbs**:

> *Mr. and Mrs. Lee are at home. It's evening, around dinner time. Mr. Lee is watching TV. Mrs. Lee walks in and says, "Dinner's ready." Mr. Lee tells her that he'll be there in a minute. Mrs. Lee warns him that the dinner is getting cold, but Mr. wants to hear the end of a news report before he has his dinner.*

Example of STUDENT B's written story, using **past tense reporting verbs**:

> *Mr. and Mrs. Lee were at home yesterday evening around dinner time. Mr. Lee was watching TV when Mrs. came into the room and told him dinner was ready. He told her he would be there in a minute, but Mrs. Lee knew her husband meant more than a minute. She got a little impatient and warned him that their dinner was getting cold. Mr. Lee didn't get up from his chair. He told his wife that he had to hear the end of a news report he was watching.*

STORY 1:

STORY 2:

STORY 3:

◇ PRACTICE 20—SELFSTUDY: Using *advise*, *suggest*, and *recommend*. (Chart 15-7)

Directions: Choose the correct completion.

1. I advised him __**A**__ more time at the library.
   A. to spend   B. spending   C. should spend

2. I advised _____ more time at the library.
   A. to spend   B. spending   C. should spend

3. I suggested _____ to the zoo.
   A. to go   B. going   C. should go

4. I suggested that we _____ to the zoo.
   A. to go   B. going   C. should go

5. Bill recommended _____ to Luigi's Restaurant.
   A. to go   B. going   C. should go

6. Bill recommended that we _____ to Luigi's Restaurant.
   A. to go   B. going   C. should go

7. My mother advised me _____ in school.
   A. to stay   B. staying   C. should stay

8. My brother advised _____ in school, too.
   A. to stay   B. staying   C. should stay

9. My father suggested that I _____ for a job.
   A. to look   B. looking   C. should look

10. My uncle suggested _____ for a job, too.
    A. to look   B. looking   C. should look

11. My sister recommended that I _____ around the world for a year.
    A. to travel   B. traveling   C. should travel

12. My aunt recommended _____ around the world for a year, too.
    A. to travel   B. traveling   C. should travel

◇ PRACTICE 21—GUIDED STUDY: Using *advise*, *suggest*, and *recommend*. (Chart 15-7)

Directions: Use the given information to complete the sentences.

1. The teacher said to Pierre, "You should spend more time on your studies."

   → The teacher advised Pierre _____**to spend**_____ more time on his studies.

2. Ms. Wah said to Anna, "You should go to Mills College."

   → Ms. Wah suggested to Anna (that) _____ to Mills College.

3. My gardening book says, "Plant tomatoes in June."

   → My gardening book recommends _____ tomatoes in June.

4. When we were planning our vacation, my wife said, "How about Argentina? Let's go there."

   → My wife suggested _____ to Argentina on our vacation.

5. Nutrition experts say, "People should eat a lot of fresh fruit."

→ Nutrition experts recommend _____ a lot of fresh fruit.

6. My field of study is geology. My sister said, "You should change your major to biology."

→ My sister advised me _____ my major to biology.

7. My brother said, "I think you should change to chemistry."

→ My brother suggested _____ my major to chemistry.

8. My aunt said, "I think you ought to change your major to business."

→ My aunt recommended _____ my major to business.

◇ PRACTICE 22—GUIDED STUDY: Reporting speech. (Charts 15-1 → 15-7)

Directions: Report on the people in the pictures and what they say. Use the formal sequence of tenses.

Example:

At the Restaurant

Possible written report:

One day Susan and Paul were at a restaurant. Susan picked up her menu and looked at it. Paul left his menu on the table. Susan asked Paul what he was going to have. He said he wasn't going to have anything (OR: was going to have nothing) because he wasn't hungry. He'd already eaten. Susan was surprised. She asked him why he had come to the restaurant with her. He told her (that) he needed to talk to her about a problem he was having at work.

Before School in the Morning

◇ PRACTICE 23—GUIDED STUDY: Questions and noun clauses. (Chapters 6, 14, and 15)

Directions: Ask questions and write reports as directed below.

STUDENT A: (1) Make up five to ten questions to ask a classmate, friend, roommate, etc.
                    (2) Ask the questions and write a report of the information you received. Then give
                          your report to STUDENT B. Don't show STUDENT B your list of questions.

STUDENT B: (3) Read STUDENT A's report. Try to figure out and write down the questions that
                          STUDENT A asked.
                    (4) Then write a report on the interview using REPORTED SPEECH. Use a separate
                          sentence to report each question. Use the formal sequence of tenses.

Example:
(1) STUDENT A's list of questions:
        1. Where do you live?
        2. How long have you been here?
        3. What is your favorite color?
        4. Are you married?
        5. What are you studying?

(2) STUDENT A's written report:

My friend Po lives in Reed Hall. He's been here for eight months. His favorite color is sky blue. He's not married. He's studying chemical engineering.

(3) STUDENT B's list of probable questions:

1. *Where do you live?*
2. *How long have you been at this school?*
3. *What's your favorite color?*
4. *Are you married?*
5. *What subject are you studying?*

(4) STUDENT B's report of the interview, using reported speech:

(Student A) asked his friend Po where he lived. He asked him how long he had been here. He wanted to know what his favorite color was. He wanted to know if he was married. And finally, he asked him what he was studying.

CHAPTER *16*
Using Wish; *Using* If

◇ PRACTICE 1—SELFSTUDY: Making wishes. (Charts 16-1 and 16-2)

Directions: Circle the correct answer, then answer the questions.

Sara, David, and Heidi are twelve years old. They're lost in the woods because they left the main path. Sara didn't listen to her mother, who told her not to come to the woods. None of them has a flashlight. It's dark.

1. Is Sara safe at home?

   YES (NO)

   What does she wish?

   → *She wishes she were safe at home.*

2. Did David come to the woods?

   YES NO

   What does he wish?

3. Can Heidi remember how to get back to town?

   YES NO

   What does she wish?

4. Did Sara listen to her mother?

   YES NO

   What does she wish?

5. Does David have a flashlight?

   YES NO

   What does he wish?

6. Did the three leave the main path?

   YES NO

   What does Heidi wish?

DAVID   SARA   HEIDI

◇ PRACTICE 2—SELFSTUDY: Making wishes. (Chart 16-1)

Directions: Using the given information, complete the sentences.

1. In truth, I _____**don't have**_____ a dog, but I really like dogs.

   I *wish* I _____**had**_____ a dog.

2. In truth, Linda _____**has**_____ a cat, but it ruins her furniture.

   She *wishes* she _____**didn't have**_____ a cat.

3. In truth, Mr. Mills _____**doesn't teach**_____ my math class. He's a good teacher.

   I *wish* Mr. Mills _____ my math class.

4. In truth, it _____**snows**_____ here in winter, and I don't like snow.

   I *wish* it _____ here in winter.

5. In truth, I _____**don't understand**_____ my friend Pierre.

   I *wish* I _____ him.

6. In truth, I _____**can't sing**_____ very well, but I like to sing.

   I *wish* I _____ well.

7. In truth, I _____**have**_____ four roommates.

   I *wish* I _____ four roommates.

   I *wish* I _____ only one roommate.

8. In truth, I _____**have to study**_____ tonight.

   I *wish* I _____ tonight.

9. In truth, I _____**am not**_____ at home with my family. I'd like to be with them.

   I *wish* I _____ at home.

10. In truth, Tom _____**isn't**_____ here. I'd like to see him.

    I *wish* he _____ here.

◇ PRACTICE 3—SELFSTUDY: Using auxiliaries after *wish*. (Charts 6-1 and 16-1)

Directions: Complete the dialogues with auxiliary verbs.

1. A: Do you have a TV set?

   B: No, I _____**don't**_____ , but I *wish* I _____**did**_____ .

2. A: Do you have a cold?

   B: Yes, I _____ , but I *wish* I _____ .

3. A: Is Bob here?

   B: No, he _____ , but I *wish* he _____ .

4. A: Does Rita speak Chinese?

   B: No, she _____ , but I *wish* she _____ .

5. A: Are you shy?

   B: Yes, I _____ , but I *wish* I _____ .

6. A: Can you stay home from work today?

   B: No, I _____ , but I *wish* I _____ .

◇ PRACTICE 4—SELFSTUDY: Making wishes about the past. (Chart 16-2)

   Directions: Using the given information, complete the sentences.

   1. In truth, I _____ **didn't have** _____ a dog when I was a child. I like dogs.

      I *wish* I _____ **had had** _____ a dog.

   2. In truth, Linda _____ **had** _____ a cat, but it ruined her furniture.

      She *wishes* she _____ **hadn't had** _____ a cat.

   3. In truth, I _____ **didn't understand** _____ Pierre's problem. I couldn't help him.

      I *wish* I _____ his problem.

   4. In truth, I _____ **lost** _____ the keys to my apartment. I couldn't get in.

      I *wish* I _____ them.

   5. In truth, I _____ **wasn't** _____ at the meeting yesterday.

      I *wish* I _____ at the meeting yesterday.

◇ PRACTICE 5—SELFSTUDY: Using auxiliaries after *wish*. (Charts 6–1, 16-1, and 16-2)

   Directions: Complete the dialogues with auxiliary verbs.

   1. A: Did you lose your keys?

      B: Yes, I _____ **did** _____ , but I wish I _____ **hadn't** _____ .

   2. A: Did you go to the party?

      B: No, I _____ , but I wish I _____ .

   3. A: Did you go to the concert?

      B: Yes, I _____ , but I wish I _____ . It was boring.

   4. A: Do you know Jennifer Hayakawa?

      B: No, I _____ , but I wish I _____ .

   5. A: Are you busy today?

      B: Yes, I _____ , but I wish I _____ .

◇ PRACTICE 6—GUIDED STUDY: Using *wish.* (Charts 16-1 and 16-2)

Directions: What do the following people probably wish?

1. *Rosa:* I don't have a bicycle. I can't ride a bike to school. I have to walk. I didn't buy a bicycle last year.

   → *Rosa wishes that she had a bicycle.*
   She wishes she could ride a bike to school.
   She wishes she . . . .

2. *Hiroki:* I can't speak Spanish. I can't understand Maria and Roberto when they speak Spanish. I didn't study Spanish in high school.

3. *Dennis:* I didn't go to the meeting last night. I didn't know about it. My boss was really angry. Bob forgot to tell me about the meeting.

4. *Linda:* I have to clean up the kitchen this morning. My roommate didn't wash the dishes last night. I can't go to the beach. I'm not at the beach in the sun right now.

◇ PRACTICE 7—SELFSTUDY: Using *if*: contrary-to-fact. (Charts 16-3 → 16-6)

Directions: Answer the questions and complete the sentences.

1. Does David have matches?   YES   (NO)

   Can they build a fire?   YES   (NO)

   But if David _____**had**_____

   matches, they _____**could build**_____

   a fire.

2. Is Sara at home?   YES   NO

   Is she afraid?   YES   NO

   But if Sara _____ at home,

   she _____ afraid.

3. Does Heidi have a flashlight?   YES   NO

   Can she lead them out of the woods?   YES   NO

   But if Heidi _____ a flashlight, she

   _____ them out of the woods.

HEIDI   DAVID   SARA

4. Did Sara listen to her mother?   YES   NO

Did she come to the woods?   YES   NO

But if Sara _____ to her mother, she _____ to the woods.

5. Did David, Heidi, and Sara leave the main path?   YES   NO

Did they get lost?   YES   NO

But if David, Heidi, and Sara _____ the main path, they _____

lost.

◇ PRACTICE 8—SELFSTUDY: Using *if:* contrary-to-fact. (Chart 16-3)

Directions: Use the given information to complete the sentences.

1. In truth, I _____**am not**_____ from Italy. I _____**can't speak**_____ Italian.

But *if* I _____**were**_____ from Italy, I _____*could speak*_____ Italian.

2. In truth, Al _____**has**_____ enough money. He_____**won't ask**_____ for a loan.

But *if* Al _____*didn't have*_____ enough money, he _____*would ask*_____ for a loan.

3. In truth, Tom _____**doesn't need**_____ a new coat. He_____**won't buy**_____ one.

But *if* Tom _____ a new coat, he _____ one.

4. In truth, Kate _____**is**_____ tired. She_____**won't finish**_____ her work.

But *if* Kate _____ tired, she_____ her work.

5. In truth, I _____**don't have**_____ a ticket. I _____**can't go**_____ to the concert.

But *if* I _____ a ticket, I_____ to the concert.

6. In truth, I _____**am not**_____ an artist. I _____**can't paint**_____ your picture.

But *if* I _____ an artist, I _____ your picture.

7. In truth, John **doesn't understand** the problem. He _____**can't solve**_____ it.

But *if* John _____ the problem, he_____ it.

◇ PRACTICE 9—GUIDED STUDY: Using *if:* contrary-to-fact. (Chart 16-3)

Directions: Answer the questions.

PART I: If you were the following, what would (or could) you do?

1. hungry → *If I were hungry, I'd eat a Big Mac.*
2. tired
3. lost in a big city
4. *(the name of someone)*
5. fluent in five languages
6. the most powerful person in the world

PART II: If you had the following things, what would (or could) you do?

7. a horse → *If I had a horse, I would ride it to school.*
8. a boat
9. six apples
10. a gun
11. a car with a phone in it
12. my own private jet airplane

PART III: If you were in the following places, what would (or could) you do?

13. in India → *If I were in India, I would visit the Taj Mahal.*
14. on a beach
15. at home right now
16. *(choose one)* Paris, Damascus, Tokyo, Rio de Janeiro
17. on a spaceship in outer space
18. *(name of a local place)*

◇ PRACTICE 10—SELFSTUDY: *If:* true vs. contrary-to-fact. (Charts 16-4 and 16-5)

Directions: Using the given information, complete the sentences with the words in parentheses.

1. I may need a new bike this year.

    If I *(need)* _____**need**_____ a new bike, I *(buy)* _____**will/can buy**_____ one.

2. I don't need a new bike this year

    However, if I *(need)* _____**needed**_____ a new bike, I *(buy)* _____**would/could buy**_____ one.

3. I didn't need a new bike last year.

    However, if I *(need)* _____**had needed**_____ a new bike last year, I *(buy)*

    _____**would have/could have bought**_____ one.

4. I may go to Japan next month.

    If I *(go)* _____ to Japan, I *(see)* _____ Yoko.

5. I won't go to Japan next week.

    However, if I *(go)* _____ to Japan, I *(see)* _____ Yoko.

6. I didn't go to Japan last month.

    However, if I *(go)* _____ to Japan last month, I *(see)* _____ Yoko.

7. I may have a pen right now.

    If I *(have)* _____ a pen, I *(write)* _____ a letter.

8. I don't have a pen right now.

    However, if I *(have)* _____ a pen, I *(write)* _____ a letter.

9. I didn't have a pen while I was waiting for my plane at the airport yesterday.

    However, if I *(have)* _____ a pen, I *(write)* _____ a letter.

◇ PRACTICE 11—SELFSTUDY: *If:* contrary-to-fact in the past. (Chart 16-5)

Directions: Using the given information, complete the sentences with the words in parentheses.

1. I didn't go to work this morning, so I didn't finish my report.

   → If I *(go)* _____**had gone**_____ to work this morning, I *(finish)* __**would/could have**__ ____**finished**____ my report.

2. I didn't hear the doorbell, so I didn't answer the door.

   → I *(answer)* _____ the door if I *(hear)* _____ _____ the doorbell.

3. You didn't tell me about your problem, so I didn't help you.

   → If you *(tell)* _____ me about your problem, I *(help)* _____ _____ you.

4. Joe didn't come with us to the Rocky Mountains, so he didn't see the beautiful scenery.

   → Joe *(see)* _____ some beautiful scenery if he *(come)* _____ with us to the Rocky Mountains.

5. Barbara didn't read the story before class, so she couldn't talk about it during the class discussion.

   → If Barbara *(read)* _____ the book before class, she *(talk)* _____ about it during the class discussion.

6. We didn't offer you a ride because we didn't see you standing near the road.

   → If we *(see)* _____ you standing near the road, we *(offer)* _____ you a ride.

7. My brother had to get a job, so he didn't complete his education.

   → If my brother *(have to get, not)* _____ a job, he *(complete)* _____ his education.

◇ PRACTICE 12—SELFSTUDY: Contracting *had* and *would.* (Charts 16-1 → 16-6)

Directions: Change the contraction with apostrophe + **d** to the full word, **HAD** or **WOULD**.

         had   **would**
1. If you'd ⌃ asked me, I'd ⌃ have told you the truth.

2. I'd be careful if I were you.

3. If I'd known that you were sick, I'd have brought you some flowers.

4. If Jack were here, he'd help us.

5. If I'd told them, they'd have laughed at me.

◇ PRACTICE 13—SELFSTUDY: Review of verb forms with *if.* (Chapter 16)

Directions: Choose the correct completion.

1. If I'd studied, I _____ the test yesterday.
   A. passed   B. had passed   C. would pass   D. would have passed

2. I'd go to the concert with you tomorrow if I _____ the time, but I'm going to be too busy.
   A. have   B. had   C. would have   D. would have had

3. If you let me know when your computer comes, I _____ you connect it .
   A. helped   B. help   C. will help   D. would help

4. If you'd listened to the radio last night, you _____ about the riot at the soccer game.
   A. heard   B. will hear   C. had heard   D. would have heard

5. I would have picked you up at the airport if you _____ me your arrival time.
   A. had told   B. would tell   C. tell   D. did tell

6. I don't mind driving, but I don't know the way. I _____ if you read the map and give me directions.
   A. drive   B. drove   C. will drive   D. would have driven

7. The weather is too cold today. If it _____ so cold, we could go swimming.
   A. isn't   B. weren't   C. hadn't been   D. wouldn't have been

8. If you _____ my baby while I go to the store, I'll get your groceries for you. Okay?
   A. watch   B. watched   C. had watched   D. would have watched

9. I would have embarrassed my parents if I _____ during the wedding ceremony.
   A. laugh   B. will laugh   C. would laugh   D. had laughed

10. You shouldn't spend all day at your desk. If you took long walks every day, you _____ better.
   A. feel   B. will feel   C. felt   D. would feel

◇ PRACTICE 14—GUIDED STUDY: Using *wish* and *if.* (Chapter 16)

Directions: Answer the questions in complete sentences.

Example: a. What do you wish were different about your room?
          → *I wish my room were larger.*

       b. What would/could you do if that were different?
          → *If my room were larger, I would put a sofa in it.*

1. a. What do you wish you had?
   b. What would/could you do if you had it/them?
2. a. Where do you wish you were?
   b. What would/could you do if you were there?
3. a. Who do you wish were here right now?
   b. What would/could you do if she/he/they were here?
4. a. What do you wish you had done yesterday/last week/last year?
   b. What would/could you have done if you had done that?
5. a. Where do you wish you had gone yesterday/last week/last year?
   b. What would/could you have done if you had gone there?
6. a. Who do you wish you had seen or talked to yesterday?
   b. What would/could you have done if you had seen or talked to her/him/them?

Directions: Read the story, and then complete the sentences with the correct form of the verbs in parentheses.

Sara, David, and Heidi decided to stop walking aimlessly in the woods. They huddled together under a tree and fell asleep. In the morning, they stayed in the same place. Over and over again, they yelled as loudly as they could, "Help! Help! We're lost! Help!"

A woman by the name of Mrs. Lark was in the woods. She was watching birds early in the morning while her husband was fishing in a nearby stream. She heard the children's cries and found them. The Larks knew the way out of the woods. The children were saved. They happily followed the Larks back to town. At last, they reached the open arms of their very worried parents.

If Mrs. Lark *(1. be, not)* _____ **hadn't been** _____ in the woods, she *(2. find, not)*

_____ the children. If the children *(3. yell, not)*

_____ or if they *(4. walk)* _____ to a

different part of the woods, Mrs. Lark *(5. hear, not)* _____

them. If the children *(6. yell, not)* _____ , they *(7. found, not)*

_____ by Mrs. Lark. If the Larks *(8. know, not)*

_____ the way out of the woods, the children *(9. have to*

spend) _____ another night there. The childen are fortunate

that Mrs. Lark likes to go birdwatching. All of the children wish they *(10. go, not)* _____

_____ into the woods alone.

◇ PRACTICE 16—GUIDED STUDY: Past verbs, true and contrary-to-fact.
(Chapters 2, 11, and 16)

Directions: Complete the sentences with the correct form of the verbs in parentheses.

Yesterday Sam *(1. have)* _____**had**_____ an automobile accident. While he *(2. drive)*

_____ down the road, a squirrel *(3. run)* _____ in front of his car.

Sam *(4. drive)* _____ off the road

to miss the squirrel. His car *(5. hit)*

_____ a tree. The squirrel *(6. run)*

_____ up the tree, so it *(7. kill, not)*

_____ by Sam's car.

Sam *(8. have, not)* _____ an automobile accident

yesterday if a squirrel *(9. run, not)* _____ in front of his car. Sam

(10. drive, not) _____ off the road if there *(11. be, not)*

_____ a squirrel in the way. If he *(12. drive, not)* _____

_____ off the road, he *(13. hit, not)* _____

a tree. If the squirrel *(14. run, not)* _____

up the tree, it *(15. kill)* _____ by Sam's car. Both Sam and the

squirrel are lucky to be alive.

◇ PRACTICE 17—SELFSTUDY: Review of verb forms with *if*. (Chapter 16)

Directions: Choose the correct completion.

1. I don't have a word processor. But if I *(have)* _____**had**_____ my own word processor, it

(take) _____**would take**_____ me less time to write papers for school.

2. I'm not a carpenter, but if I *(be)* _____ , I *(build)* _____
my own house.

3. Pluto is the farthest planet from the sun. If you *(be)* _____ on Pluto right now,
the sun *(look)* _____ like a bright star.

4. Watching a fish tank can be relaxing. Most people begin to relax if they *(watch)*
_____ fish swimming in a tank.

5. If you light a candle on earth, the flame *(be)* _____ oval. If, however, you were
in outer space and lit a candle, the flame *(be)* _____ perfectly round.

6. Ten percent of the earth's surface is covered with ice. If the world's ice caps melted
completely, the sea level *(rise)* _____ enough to put half of the cities
in the world completely under water.

7. A: The colors of the rainbow are not all mixed together. But if the colors in a rainbow *(be)*
_____ all mixed together, what color *(the rainbow, be)* _____
_____?

   B: Purple?

   A: No. It *(be)* _____ gray.

8. A: If you rub onion juice on your skin, insects *(stay)* _____ away. It's true!
Didn't you know that?

   B: Listen, if I rubbed onion juice on myself, my wife *(stay)* _____
away from me forever! Are you trying to fool me?

9. Right now there is not a fire in this room, but think for a second. What *(you, do)*
_____ if there *(be)* _____ a fire in this room? *(you,
run)* _____ out of the room? *(you, call)* _____
the fire department? *(you, use)* _____ a fire extinguisher?

10. Mike bought a used car. While he was cleaning under the seats this morning, he found a bag
full of money. What should he do? What *(you, do)* _____ if you *(be)*
_____ Mike?

11. A: What would you be able to do if you *(have)* _____ three hands? Use your
imagination.

   B: That's a strange question. Let me see. If I *(have)* _____ three hands, I
(carry) _____ my tray at the cafeteria with two hands and *(pick)*
_____ up food with the other. Hmmm. That would be
convenient.

12. A: I wonder how long it would take me to get to one million by

adding one, plus one, plus one and so on using my

calculator.

B: If you entered a thousand ones an hour, it

(take) _____ you a

thousand hours to get to a million.

◇ PRACTICE 18—GUIDED STUDY: Conditional sentences. (Chapter 16)

Directions: Talk about wishes and "if's." Use the suggested topics or make up your own.

STUDENT A: Finish the sentence **"I wish . . . ."**
STUDENT B: Create a sentence with *if*. Imagine what would happen if STUDENT A's wish came true.

Example: dorm life
STUDENT A: *I wish I had a pet bird in my dorm room.*
STUDENT B: *If you had a pet bird in your dorm room, you'd get in trouble with the dorm manager. It's against the rules to have pets in dorm rooms.*

Example: peace
STUDENT A: *I wish there were peace throughout the world.*
STUDENT B: *If there were peace throughout the world, everybody would be very happy.*

Suggested topics to make wishes about:

1. this school
2. food
3. the world
4. a skill you'd like to have
5. language
6. sports

7. season of the year
8. money
9. friends
10. weather
11. the environment
12. etc.

◇ PRACTICE 19—GUIDED STUDY: Conditional sentences. (Chapter 16)

Directions: Discuss or write about the following topics.

1. If you could live in a different time period, which would you choose?
2. If you could ask (*name of a world leader*) one question, what would you say? Why? What do you think the answer would be?
3. If you had only two career choices—to be an artist or to be a scientist—which would you choose and why?
4. What would the earth be like today if there were no humans and never had been any?

Index

Go + -ing (go shopping), 198

Answer Key

Answers to the Selfstudy Practices

Chapter 9 CONNECTING IDEAS

◇ PRACTICE 1, p. 175.

NOUN + NOUN + NOUN
1. The farmer has a <u>cow</u>, a <u>goat</u>, and a black <u>horse</u>.

ADJ + ADJ
2. Danny is a <u>bright</u> and <u>happy</u> child.

VERB + VERB
3. I <u>picked</u> up the telephone and <u>dialed</u> Steve's number.

VERB + VERB
4. The cook <u>washed</u> the vegetables and <u>put</u> them in boiling water.

ADJ + ADJ
5. My feet were <u>cold</u> and <u>wet</u>.

ADJ + ADJ + ADJ
6. Sara is <u>responsible</u>, <u>considerate</u>, and <u>trustworthy</u>.

NOUN + NOUN + NOUN
7. The three largest land animals are the <u>elephant</u>, the <u>rhinoceros</u>, and the <u>hippopotamus</u>.

VERB + VERB
8. A hippopotamus <u>rests</u> in water during the day and <u>feeds</u> on land at night.

◇ PRACTICE 2, p. 176.

1. Rivers**,** streams**,** lakes**,** and oceans are all bodies of water.
2. My oldest brother**,** my neighbor**,** and I went shopping yesterday.
3. Ms. Parker is intelligent**,** friendly**,** and kind.
4. Did you bring copies of the annual report for Sue**,** Dan**,** Joe**,** and Mary?
5. In the early 1600s, the Chinese made wallpaper by painting birds**,** flowers**,** and landscapes on large sheets of rice paper.
6. Can you watch television**,** listen to the radio**,** and read the newspaper at the same time?
7. Lawyers**,** doctors**,** teachers**,** and accountants all have some form of continuing education throughout their careers.
8. Gold is beautiful**,** workable**,** indestructible**,** and rare.
9. My mother**,** father**,** grandfather**,** and sisters welcomed my brother and me home.
10. My husband imitates sounds for our children. He moos like a cow**,** roars like a lion**,** and barks like a dog.

◇ PRACTICE 4, p. 177.

S V S V
1. Birds fly**,** and fish swim.

S V S V
2. Birds fly**.** Fish swim.

S V S V
3. Dogs bark**.** Lions roar.

S V S V
4. Dogs bark**,** and lions roar.

S V S V
5. A week has seven days**.** A year has 365 days.

S V S V
6. A week has seven days**,** and a year has 365 days.

S V S V
7. Bill raised his hand**,** and the teacher pointed at him.

S V S V
8. Bill raised his hand**.** The teacher pointed at him.

◇ PRACTICE 5, p. 177.

1. I talked to Amy for a long time**,** but she didn't listen.
2. *(no change)*
3. I talked to Bob for a long time**,** and he listened carefully to every word.
4. *(no change)*
5. *(no change)*
6. Please call Jane**,** Ted**,** or Anna.
7. Please call Jane**,** Ted**,** and Anna.
8. I waved at my friend**,** but she didn't see me.
9. I waved at my friend**,** and she waved back.
10. *(no change)*
11. *(no change)*
12. My test was short and easy**,** but Ali's test was hard.

◇ PRACTICE 6, p. 178.
1. so
2. and
3. but
4. or
5. and
6. so
7. but
8. or

◇ PRACTICE 7, p. 178.
1. *(no change)*
2. I washed the dishes, and my son dried them.
3. I called their house, but no one answered the phone.
4. *(no change)*
5. I bought some apples, peaches, and bananas.
6. I was hungry, so I ate an apple.
7. *(no change)*
8. *(no change)*
9. My daughter is affectionate, shy, independent, and smart.
10. It started to rain, so we went inside and watched television.

◇ PRACTICE 8, p. 179.
1. Gina wants a job as an air traffic controller. Every air traffic controller worldwide uses English, so it is important for her to be fluent in the language.
2. *(no change)*
3. Mozart was a great composer, but he had a short and difficult life. During the last part of his life, he was penniless, sick, and unable to find work, but he wrote music of lasting beauty and joy.
4. Nothing in nature stays the same forever. Today's land, sea, climate, plants, and animals are all part of a relentless process of change continuing through millions of years.
5. *(no change)*
6. According to one researcher, the twenty-five most common words in English are: the, and, a, to, of, I, in, was, that, it, he, you, for, had, is, with, she, has, on, at, have, but, me, my, and not.

◇ PRACTICE 9, p. 179.
1. There are over 100,000 kinds of flies. They live throughout the world.
2. I like to get mail from my friends and family. It is important to me.
3. We are all connected by our humanity. We need to help each other. We can all live in peace.
4. There was a bad flood in Hong Kong. The streets became raging streams. Luckily no one died in the flood.
5. People have used needles since prehistoric times. The first buttons appeared more than two thousand years ago. Zippers are a relatively recent invention. The zipper was invented in 1890.

◇ PRACTICE 12, p. 182.
Part I:
1. don't
2. is
3. won't
4. don't
5. does
6. aren't
7. can
8. hasn't
9. is
10. doesn't

Part II:
11. do
12. are
13. isn't
14. didn't
15. does
16. won't
17. is
18. can't

◇ PRACTICE 13, p. 183.
1. does
2. don't
3. can't
4. don't
5. can't
6. is
7. does
8. did
9. is
10. isn't

◇ PRACTICE 14, p. 183.
Part I:
1. are too
2. can't either
3. do too
4. does too
5. doesn't either
6. isn't either
7. is too
8. wasn't either
9. didn't either
10. couldn't either
11. did too
12. can't either
13. does too
14. would too

Part II:
15. so is
16. neither do
17. neither did
18. so are
19. so do
20. neither do
21. so is
22. neither is
23. so does
24. so is
25. neither have
26. so did
27. neither did
28. neither can

◇ PRACTICE 17, p. 186.

1. Johnny was late for work because [he] [missed] the bus.
                                       S   V

2. I closed the door because [the room] [was] cold.
                      S   V

3. Because [I] [lost] my umbrella, I got wet on the way home.
        S   V

4. Joe didn't bring his book to class because [he] [couldn't find] it.
        S   V

◇ PRACTICE 18, p. 186.

1. I opened the window because the room was hot. **W**e felt more comfortable then.
2. *(no change)*
3. Because his coffee was cold, Jack didn't finish it. **H**e left it on the table and walked away.
4. Annie is very young. **B**ecause she is afraid of the dark, she likes to have a light on in her bedroom at night.
5. *(no change)*
6. Marilyn has a cold. **B**ecause she's not feeling well today, she's not going to go to her office.

◇ PRACTICE 20, p. 187.

Part I:
1. Jack never showed up for work on time, so he lost his job.
2. I was sleepy, so I took a nap.
3. The room was hot, so I opened the window.
4. It was raining, so I stayed indoors.

Part II:
5. Because Jason was hungry, he ate. OR: Jason ate because he was hungry.
6. Because I was tired, I went to bed.
7. We can't go swimming because the water in the river is polluted.
8. I was late for my job interview because my watch is broken.

◇ PRACTICE 22, p. 188.

1. B	7. B
2. B	8. B
3. A	9. A
4. B	10. A
5. A	11. B
6. A	12. A

◇ PRACTICE 23, p. 189.

1. C
2. C
3. C
4. B
5. C

◇ PRACTICE 24, p. 189.

1. C
2. A
3. A
4. B
5. C

◇ PRACTICE 27, p. 192.

1. separable
2. nonseparable
3. separable
4. nonseparable
5. separable
6. nonseparable
7. separable
8. separable

◇ PRACTICE 28, p. 193.

1. out	7. up
2. on	8. on
3. up	9. up
4. over	10. up
5. in	11. down . . . off
6. up	

◇ PRACTICE 29, p. 193.

1. on	6. away
2. up	7. A: down B: up
3. down . . . up	8. out . . . out
4. off	9. A: up B: off
5. B: on A: off	

◇ PRACTICE 30, p. 195.

1. over it — NONSEP	6. it out — SEP
2. it up — SEP	7. them off — SEP
3. it off — SEP	8. on her — NONSEP
4. them down — SEP	9. them off — SEP
5. into him — NONSEP	10. it away — SEP

◇ PRACTICE 31, p. 195.

1. over it
2. them off
3. it up . . . it down
4. them away
5. it on
6. into him
7. up . . . them down . . . into
8. B: it away . . . on me   A: it up
9. off . . . on

Chapter 10   GERUNDS AND INFINITIVES

◇ PRACTICE 1, p. 197.

1. (INF) Ann promised <u>to wait</u> for me.
2. (GER) I kept <u>walking</u> even though I was tired.
3. (INF) Alex offered <u>to help</u> me.
4. (GER) Karen finished <u>writing</u> a letter and went to bed.
5. (INF) Don't forget <u>to call</u> me tomorrow.
6. (GER) David was afraid of <u>falling</u> and <u>hurting</u> himself.
7. (GER) <u>Working</u> in a coal mine is a dangerous job.
8. (INF) It is easy <u>to grow</u> vegetables.

◇ PRACTICE 3, p. 198.

1. went dancing
2. is going to go hiking
3. went shopping
4. go swimming
5. goes fishing
6. go sightseeing
7. go camping
8. go sailing/boating
9. go skiing
10. went skydiving

◇ PRACTICE 4, p. 199.

1. B	9. A	17. B
2. A	10. A	18. B
3. B	11. A	19. A
4. B	12. B	20. B
5. A	13. B	21. B
6. B	14. B	22. B
7. B	15. A	23. B
8. B	16. B	24. A

◇ PRACTICE 5, p. 200.

1. B	8. B
2. A, B	9. A
3. A, B	10. A, B
4. B	11. A, B
5. A, B	12. A, B
6. A, B	13. B
7. A, B	14. B

◇ PRACTICE 8, p. 203.

1. Not yet. But I'm going to ~~pay the electric bill~~.
2. I didn't want to ~~go to class this morning~~.
3. No, but I ought to ~~call my mother~~.
4. No, I haven't, but I intend to ~~take my vacation~~.

◇ PRACTICE 10, p. 204.

1. in telling	14. for lying
2. of having to be	15. on paying
3. of drowning	16. of jogging
4. about meeting	17. for causing
5. for helping	18. at remembering
6. in going	19. about quitting
7. in solving	20. from doing
8. about visiting	21. into forgiving
9. of chewing	22. on eating
10. about pleasing	23. for spilling
11. on reading	24. of failing
12. to taking	25. of losing
13. like telling	

◇ PRACTICE 12, p. 206.

1. by holding
2. by reading
3. by telling
4. by watching
5. by running
6. by staying . . . taking
7. by treating

◇ PRACTICE 14, p. 208.

1. with a broom
2. with a needle and thread
3. with a saw
4. with a thermometer
5. with a spoon
6. with a key
7. with a shovel
8. with a hammer
9. with a knife
10. with a pair of scissors

◇ PRACTICE 15, p. 208.

1. with
2. by
3. with
4. by
5. by
6. with
7. by
8. by
9. with
10. with
11. by
12. with
13. by
14. with
15. with
16. with

◇ PRACTICE 16, p. 209.

1. a. It is . . . to learn	b. Learning . . . is
2. a. Eating . . . is	b. It is . . . to eat
3. a. Driving . . . is	b. It is . . . to drive
4. a. It is . . . to swim	b. Swimming . . . is
5. a. Is it . . . to live	b. Is living
6. a. Is it . . . to complete	b. Is completing

◇ PRACTICE 21, p. 211.

1. (E) I called the hotel desk (in order) to ask for an extra pillow.
2. (C) I turned on the radio (in order) to listen to a ball game.
3. (D) I looked in the encyclopedia (in order) to find the population of Malaysia.
4. (A) People wear boots (in order) to keep their feet warm and dry.
5. (I) Andy went to Egypt (in order) to see the ancient pyramids.
6. (B) Ms. Lane stood on tiptoe (in order) to reach the top shelf.
7. (J) The dentist moved the light closer to my face (in order) to look into my mouth.
8. (F) I clapped my hands and yelled (in order) to chase a stray dog away.
9. (H) Maria took a walk in the park (in order) to get some fresh air and exercise.
10. (G) I offered my cousin some money (in order) to help him pay the rent.

◇ PRACTICE 22, p. 211.

1. for
2. to
3. to
4. for
5. to
6. to
7. for
8. for
9. to
10. for
11. to
12. for

◇ PRACTICE 23, p. 212.
1. strong enough to lift
2. too weak to lift
3. too full to hold
4. large enough to hold
5. too busy to answer
6. early enough to get
7. too big to get
8. big enough to hold

◇ PRACTICE 24, p. 213.
1. Alan is **too** smart _/_ to make that kind of mistake.
2. Alan is _/_ smart **enough** to understand how to solve that problem.
3. My pocket is _/_ big **enough** to hold my wallet.
4. A horse is **too** big _/_ for a person to lift.
5. This room is **too** hot _/_ .
6. That watch is **too** expensive _/_ .
7. Are you _/_ tall **enough** to reach that book for me?
8. He's _/_ strong **enough** to lift it.
9. I am **too** busy _/_ to help you right now.
10. I think this problem is _/_ important **enough** to require our immediate attention.
11. Nora is not **too** tired _/_ to finish the project before she goes home.
12. Our company is _/_ successful **enough** to start several new branches overseas.

◇ PRACTICE 25, p. 214.
1. to remember
2. catching
3. (in order) to look
4. to go swimming
5. (in order) to invite
6. going
7. listening
8. drawing
9. to understand . . . to improve . . . to be . . . Lecturing
10. to feed
11. to feed . . . getting
12. feeding
13. to earn . . . to take
14. to take
15. to get . . . (to) sleep
16. staring . . . thinking . . . to be
17. to work . . . to go/going . . . looking . . . doing

◇ PRACTICE 26, p. 215.
1. Jim offered <u>to help</u> me with my work.
2. My son isn't old enough <u>to stay</u> home alone.
3. Do you enjoy <u>being</u> alone sometimes, or do you prefer <u>to be</u> with other people all the time?
4. I called my friend <u>to thank</u> her for the lovely gift.
5. Mary talked about <u>going</u> downtown tomorrow, but I'd like <u>to stay</u> home.
6. It is interesting <u>to learn</u> about earthquakes.
7. Approximately one million earthquakes occur around the world in a year's time. Six thousand can be felt by humans. Of those, one hundred and twenty are strong enough <u>to cause</u> serious damage to buildings, and twenty are violent enough <u>to destroy</u> a city.

8. It's important <u>to respect</u> the power of nature. A recent earthquake destroyed a bridge in California. It took five years for humans <u>to build</u> the bridge. It took nature fifteen seconds <u>to knock</u> it down.
9. <u>Predicting</u> earthquakes is difficult. I read about one scientist who tries <u>to predict</u> earthquakes by <u>reading</u> the daily newspaper's lost-and-found ads for lost pets. He believes that animals can sense an earthquake before it comes. He thinks they then begin <u>to act</u> strangely. Dogs and cats respond to the threat by <u>running</u> away to a safer place. By <u>counting</u> the number of ads for lost pets, he expects <u>to be</u> able <u>to predict</u> when an earthquake will occur.

◇ PRACTICE 29, p. 219.
1. back
2. down/off
3. out
4. away
5. on
6. down . . off
7. back
8. up
9. out . . . off . . . back/up

◇ PRACTICE 30, p. 220.
1. them away
2. it up
3. them on
4. it down
5. him up
6. it out
7. it back
8. it up
9. her back
10. it off
11. it off
12. it back
13. her out
14. it back

Chapter 11   THE PASSIVE

◇ PRACTICE 1, p. 221.
1. ACTIVE: Farmers <u>grow</u> corn.
2. PASSIVE: Corn <u>is grown</u> by farmers.
3. ACTIVE: Sara <u>wrote</u> the letter.
4. PASSIVE: The letter <u>was written</u> by Sara.
5. ACTIVE: The teacher <u>explained</u> the lesson.
6. PASSIVE: The lesson <u>was explained</u> by the teacher.
7. PASSIVE: Bridges <u>are designed</u> by engineers.
8. ACTIVE: Engineers <u>design</u> bridges.
9. ACTIVE: The mouse <u>ate</u> the cheese.
10. PASSIVE: The cheese <u>was eaten</u> by the mouse.

◇ PRACTICE 2, p. 222.
1. brought
2. built
3. bought
4. eaten
5. planned
6. given
7. grown
8. hit
9. hurt
10. left
11. lost
12. made
13. found
14. played
15. read
16. saved
17. sent
18. spoken

19. spent   23. visited
20. taken   24. worn
21. taught   25. written
22. gone   26. done

◇ PRACTICE 3, p. 222.

1. was eaten
2. is spoken
3. are written
4. was hurt
5. is going to be visited
6. has been read
7. will be played
8. can be taught
9. are going to be taken
10. have been grown
11. is worn
12. will be built

◇ PRACTICE 4, p. 223.

Part I:
1. are collected
2. are eaten
3. is grown
4. am paid
5. are written
6. is understood

Part II:
7. were collected
8. was built
9. was written
10. were destroyed

Part III:
11. have been visited
12. has been spoken
13. have been read
14. has been worn

Part IV:
15. will be discovered
16. will be visited

Part V:
17. is going to be hurt
18. are going to be offered
19. are going to be saved
20. is going to be elected

◇ PRACTICE 5, p. 224.

1. The government collects taxes.
2. Big fish eat small fish.
3. Everyone understands the meaning of a smile.
4. Leo Tolstoy wrote *War and Peace.*
5. Millions of tourists have visited the pyramids in Egypt.
6. Scientists in the twenty-first century will discover new information about the universe. OR
   Scientists will discover new information about the universe in the twenty-first century.

◇ PRACTICE 6, p. 225.

1. Mr. Rice signed the letter.
2. Did Mr. Foster sign the letter?
3. Ms. Owens sent the fax.
4. Did Mr. Chu send the other fax?
5. Will Mr. Berg meet Adam at the airport?
6. Mrs. Berg will meet Adam at the airport.
7. Has Mrs. Jordan invited you to the reception?
8. Mr. Lee invited me to the reception.
9. Is the teacher going to collect the homework?
10. The teacher is going to collect the homework.

◇ PRACTICE 8, p. 225.

1. TRANSITIVE: Alex wrote a letter.
2. INTRANSITIVE

3. INTRANSITIVE
4. INTRANSITIVE
5. TRANSITIVE: Kate caught the ball.
6. INTRANSITIVE
7. INTRANSITIVE
8. TRANSITIVE: A falling tree hit my car.
9. TRANSITIVE: I returned the book to the library yesterday.
10. INTRANSITIVE

◇ PRACTICE 9, p. 226.

1. A noise awakened me.   I was awakened by a noise.
2. (no change)
3. Alice discovered the mistake. The mistake was discovered by Alice.
4. (no change)
5. (no change)
6. (no change)
7. (no change)
8. In the fairy tale, a princess kissed a frog. In the fairy tale, a frog was kissed by a princess.
9. (no change)
10. Anita fixed the chair. The chair was fixed by Anita.
11. (no change)
12. Did the Koreans invent gunpowder? Was gunpowder invented by the Koreans?
13. (no change)
14. Research scientists will discover a cure for AIDS someday.
    A cure for AIDS will be discovered someday.   OR
    A cure for AIDS will someday be discovered.
15. (no change)

◇ PRACTICE 10, p. 227.

1. *unknown*
2. The wastebasket was emptied by Fred. Fred
3. Paul
4. The Eiffel Tower was designed by Alexandre Eiffel.
   Alexandre Eiffel
5. *unknown*
6. Nicole
7. *unknown*
8. Our exam papers will be corrected by Ms. Brown. Ms. Brown
9. *unknown*
10. Sara
11. *unknown*
12. *unknown*

◇ PRACTICE 12, p. 229.

1. enjoys
2. was established . . . established . . . were established
3. were disgusted . . . were replaced . . . were studied . . . (were) kept . . . became
4. understood . . . have become . . . was reduced . . . would become . . . believe
5. are now put . . . are watched . . . are fed . . . have
6. is prepared . . . is designed . . . are fed . . . are fed
7. are treated

◇ PRACTICE 13, p. 230.

1. Some people are considering a new plan.
   . . . is being considered
2. The grandparents are watching the children.
   . . . are being watched
3. Some painters are painting Mr. Rivera's apartment this week.
   . . . is being painted
4. Many of the older people in the neighborhood were growing vegetables.
   . . . were being grown
5. Eric's cousins are meeting him at the airport this afternoon.
   . . . is being met
6. I watched while the movers were moving the furniture from my apartment to a truck.
   . . . was being moved

◇ PRACTICE 16, p. 232.

1. must be sent
2. can be found
3. ought to be washed
4. can be cooked or (can be) eaten
5. has to be fixed
6. might be destroyed
7. may be called off
8. must be kept
9. shouldn't be pronounced
10. should be removed

◇ PRACTICE 18, p. 233.

1. are loved . . . brings . . . are often used . . . can be found
2. exist . . . can be found . . . have
3. are carried . . . carries . . . have been introduced
4. are appreciated . . . is made . . . is gathered . . . are eaten
5. are made . . . do not come . . . are made
6. may be planted . . . (may be) grown . . . survive

◇ PRACTICE 20, p. 235.

1. scare
2. are scared of
3. interest
4. is interested in
5. disappoint
6. are disappointed in
7. is pleased with
8. pleases
9. satisfies
10. am satisfied with

◇ PRACTICE 21, p. 236.

1. interesting
2. interested
3. exciting
4. excited
5. fascinated
6. fascinating
7. bored and confused
8. boring and confusing
9. interesting
10. fascinating . . . surprising

◇ PRACTICE 24, p. 238.

1. got sunburned
2. get well
3. get married
4. gets hungry
5. gets dark
6. get invited
7. get dry
8. getting tired
9. got dressed
10. get busy
11. get dizzy
12. got wet

◇ PRACTICE 26, p. 240.

1. B, C
2. A
3. B, C
4. A
5. B, C
6. A

◇ PRACTICE 27, p. 240.

1. used to go
2. am used to going/am accustomed to going
3. used to eat
4. is used to growing/is accustomed to growing
5. is used to eating/is accustomed to eating
6. used to have
7. am used to taking/am accustomed to taking
8. used to go

◇ PRACTICE 29, p. 241.

1. I'm supposed *to* call my parents tonight.
2. We're not suppose*d* to tell anyone about the surprise.
3. You *aren't* supposed to talk to Alan about the surprise.
4. My friend was suppose*d* to call me last night, but he didn't.
5. Children *are* supposed to respect their parents.
6. *Weren't* you supposed *to* be at the meeting last night?

◇ PRACTICE 30, p. 241.

1. (H) Doctors are supposed to care about their patients.
2. (C) Visitors at a zoo are not supposed to feed the animals.
3. (E) Employees are supposed to be on time for work.
4. (B) Air passengers are supposed to buckle their seatbelts before takeoff.
5. (D) Theatergoers are not supposed to talk during a performance.
6. (I) Soldiers on sentry duty are not supposed to fall asleep.
7. (A) Children are supposed to listen to their parents.
8. (J) Heads of state are supposed to be diplomatic.
9. (F) A dog is supposed to obey its trainer.
10. (G) People who live in apartments are supposed to pay their rent on time.

Chapter 12 ADJECTIVE CLAUSES

◇ PRACTICE 1, p. 245.
1. I thanked the man <u>who helped me move the refrigerator</u>.
   I thanked the man.
   He helped me move the refrigerator.
2. A woman <u>who was wearing a gray suit</u> asked me for directions.
   1: A woman asked me for directions.
   2: She was wearing a gray suit.
3. I saw a man <u>who was wearing a blue coat</u>.
   1: I saw a man.
   2: He was wearing a blue coat.
4. The woman <u>who aided the rebels</u> put her life in danger.
   1: The woman put her life in danger.
   2: She aided the rebels.
5. I know some people <u>who live on a boat</u>.
   1: I know some people.
   2: They live on a boat.

◇ PRACTICE 2, p. 246.
1. The woman <u>who answered the phone</u> was polite.
2. The man <u>who sang at the concert</u> has a good voice.
3. We enjoyed the actors <u>who played the leading roles</u>.
4. The girl <u>who fell down the stairs</u> is hurt.

◇ PRACTICE 3, p. 247.
1. The man **who** answered the phone was polite.
2. I liked the people **who** sat next to us at the soccer game.
3. People **who** paint houses for a living are called house painters.
4. I'm uncomfortable around married couples **who** argue all the time.
5. While I was waiting at the bus stop, I stood next to an elderly gentleman **who** started a conversation with me about my educational plans.

◇ PRACTICE 4, p. 247.
1. The people <u>who live next to me</u> are nice.   2: They live next to me.
   S V
2. The people <u>whom Kate visited yesterday</u> were French.
   S V
   2: Kate visited them yesterday
3. The people <u>whom I saw at the park</u> were having a picnic.   2: I saw them at the park.
4. The students <u>who go to this school</u> are friendly.
   2: They go to this school.
5. The woman <u>whom you met last week</u> lives in Mexico.   2: You met her last week.

◇ PRACTICE 5, p. 248.
1. The woman <u>whom Jack met</u> was polite.
2. I like the woman <u>who manages my uncle's store</u>.
3. The singer <u>whom we heard at the concert</u> was wonderful.
4. The people <u>who came to dinner</u> brought a small gift.
5. What is the name of the woman <u>whom Tom invited to the dance</u>?

◇ PRACTICE 6, p. 248.
1. who
2. who(m)
3. who
4. who(m)
5. who
6. who(m)
7. who
8. who(m)

◇ PRACTICE 8, p. 249.
1. ~~that~~
2. (no change)
3. ~~that~~
4. ~~that~~
5. (no change)
6. (no change) . . . ~~that~~

◇ PRACTICE 9, p. 250.
1. who
   that
2. who(m)
   that
   Ø
3. who(m)
   that
   Ø
4. who
   that
5. who
   that
6. who(m)
   that
   Ø

◇ PRACTICE 10, p. 250.
1. C
2. A
3. C
4. C
5. B
6. A

◇ PRACTICE 11, p. 251.
1. which
   that
   Ø
2. which
   that
3. which
   that
   Ø
4. which
   that
5. which
   that
   Ø
6. which
   that

◇ PRACTICE 12, p. 251.
1. ~~them~~
2. ~~it~~
3. ~~her~~
4. ~~it~~
5. ~~it~~
6. ~~her~~

◇ PRACTICE 15, p. 253.
1. A, C, D
2. A, D
3. C, D, E
4. A, C, D
5. A, D
6. C, D
7. C, D, E
8. C, D

◇ PRACTICE 20, p. 256.
1. <u>tool</u> . . . is
2. <u>tools</u> . . . are
3. <u>woman</u> . . . lives
4. <u>people</u> . . . live
5. <u>cousin</u> . . . works
6. <u>coal miners</u> . . . work
7. <u>athlete</u> . . . plays
8. <u>athletes</u> . . . play
9. <u>person</u> . . . makes
10. <u>artists</u> . . . make

◇ PRACTICE 21, p. 257.
1. that . . . for
   which . . . for
   Ø . . . for
   for which . . . Ø
2. that . . . to
   which . . . to
   Ø . . . to
   to which . . . Ø
3. that . . . in
   which . . . in
   Ø . . . in
   in which . . . Ø
4. that . . . with
   who(m) . . . with
   Ø . . . with
   with whom . . . Ø

◇ PRACTICE 23, p. 258.
1. a. to   b. [we listened **to** at Sara's apartment]
2. a. Ø   b. [I accidentally broke **Ø**]
3. a. for   b. [we were waiting **for**]
4. a. to   b. [I always enjoy **to** about politics]
5. a. Ø   b. [I had just written **Ø**]
6. a. in   b. [I've been interested **in** for a long time]

◇ PRACTICE 24, p. 258.
1. [I was looking **at**]
2. [I wanted **Ø**]
3. [we were listening **to** at Jim's yesterday]
4. [I was staring **at**]
5. [I've always been able to depend **on**]
6. [I was carrying **Ø**]
7. [that I'm not familiar **with**]
8. [we talked **about** in class]
9. [she is arguing **with**]
10. [they ate **Ø** at the cafe]
11. [you waved **at**]
12. [I borrowed money **from**]

◇ PRACTICE 26, p. 259.
1. I know a man <u>whose daughter is a pilot</u>.
   I know a man. His daughter is a pilot.
2. The woman <u>whose husband is out of work</u> found a job at Mel's Diner.
   The woman found a job at Mel's Diner. Her husband is out of work.
3. The man <u>whose wallet I found</u> gave me a reward.
   The man gave me a reward. I found his wallet.

4. I know a girl <u>whose family never sits down and eats dinner together</u>.
   I know a girl. Her family never sits down and eats dinner together.
5. The people <u>whose window I broke</u> got really angry.
   The people got really angry. I broke their window.

◇ PRACTICE 27, p. 261.
1. whose son was in an accident
2. James chose for his bedroom walls
3. I slept on at the hotel last night
4. that/which is used to carry boats with goods and/or passengers
5. whose children were doing poorly in her class
6. Ted bought for his wife on their anniversary
7. whose views I share
8. that/which had backbones
9. that/which disrupted the global climate and caused mass extinctions of animal life

◇ PRACTICE 29, p. 262.
1. who/that
2. that/which/Ø
3. who/that
4. whose
5. that/which
6. who(m)/that/Ø
7. that/which
8. whose

◇ PRACTICE 31, p. 264.
1. (Flowers) that bloom year after year are called perennials. (Flowers) that bloom only one season are called annuals.
2. B: Are you talking about the (boy) who's wearing the striped shirt or the (boy) who has on the T-shirt?
   A: I'm talking about the (boy) who just waved at us . . . . Do you see the (kid) that has the red baseball cap?
3. . . . . He stayed with a (family) who lived near Quito, Ecuador . . . . At first, all the (things) they did and said seemed strange to Hiroki . . . . He felt homesick for (people) who were like him in their customs and habits. But as time went on, he began to appreciate the way of (life) that his host family followed. Many of the (things) Hiroki did with his host family began to feel natural to him . . . . At the beginning of his stay in Ecuador, he had noticed only the (things) that were different between his host family and himself.
   At the end, he understood how many (things) they had in common as human beings despite their differences in cultural background.
4. Many of the (problems) that exist today have existed since the beginning of recorded history. One of these problems is violent conflict between (people) who come from different geographical areas or cultural backgrounds. One group may distrust and fear another group of (people) who are different from themselves in language, customs, politics, religion, and/or appearance. These irrational fears are the source of much of the (violence) that has occurred throughout the history of the world.

PRACTICE 34, p. 266.
1. up
2. out
3. in
4. out
5. over
6. down
7. over
8. out
9. up
10. out/in
11. out
12. up

PRACTICE 35, p. 267.
1. out for
2. in on
3. up in
4. along with
5. around with
6. out of
7. through with
8. out for
9. back from
10. out of

Chapter 13   COMPARISONS

PRACTICE 1, p. 268.
1. aren't as noisy as
2. is as lazy as
3. aren't as strong as
4. is as tall as
5. isn't as comfortable as
6. was as nervous as
7. isn't as big as
8. isn't as fresh and clean as
9. am not as ambitious as
10. are more interesting than

PRACTICE 2, p. 269.
Part I:
1. almost as/not quite as
2. not nearly as
3. just as
4. almost as/not quite as

Part II:
5. just as
6. not nearly as
7. almost as/not quite as
8. almost as/not quite as

Part III:
9. just as
10. not nearly as
11. almost as/not quite as

Part IV:
12. just as
13. almost as/not quite as
14. just as
15. not nearly as
16. almost as/not quite as

PRACTICE 4, p. 271.
1. E
2. C
3. D
4. G
5. B
6. H
7. F
8. A

PRACTICE 5, p. 271.
1. stronger, strongest
2. more important, most important
3. softer, softest
4. lazier, laziest
5. more wonderful, most wonderful
6. calmer, calmest
7. tamer, tamest
8. dimmer, dimmest
9. more convenient, most convenient
10. cleverer, cleverest OR more clever, most clever
11. better, best
12. worse, worst
13. farther/further, farthest/furthest
14. slower, slowest
15. more slowly, most slowly

PRACTICE 7, p. 273.
1. softer
2. colder
3. more expensive
4. cleaner
5. prettier
6. more careful
7. funnier
8. more confusing
9. more generous
10. worse
11. thinner
12. lazier

PRACTICE 9, p. 275.
1. A, B
2. B
3. A, B
4. A, B
5. B
6. B
7. A, B
8. B
9. A, B
10. B

PRACTICE 11, p. 276.
1. I did
2. she is
3. I do
4. she did
5. I was
6. he will
7. he does
8. he has
9. she did
10. he can

PRACTICE 13, p. 277.
1. A
2. B, C, D
3. A
4. B, C, D
5. B, C, D
6. A
7. B, C, D
8. A

PRACTICE 14, p. 277.
1. A, B
2. B
3. B
4. A, B
5. A, B
6. A, B
7. B
8. A, B

PRACTICE 16, p. 278.
1. more slowly - ADV
2. slower - ADJ
3. more serious - ADJ
4. more seriously - ADV
5. more politely - ADV
6. more polite - ADJ
7. more careful - ADJ
8. more carefully - ADV
9. more clearly - ADV
10. clearer - ADJ

◇ PRACTICE 17, p. 279.

1. more newspapers - NOUN
2. more homework - NOUN
3. more snow - NOUN
4. more friends - NOUN
5. more pleasant - ADJ
6. more easily - ADV
7. more books - NOUN
8. more carefully - ADJ
9. louder - ADJ

◇ PRACTICE 19, p. 280.

1. faster and faster
2. angrier and angrier
   [also possible: more and more angry]
3. bigger and bigger
4. colder and colder
5. better and better
6. harder and harder . . . wetter and wetter
7. weaker and weaker

◇ PRACTICE 20, p. 281.

1. The fresher . . . the better
2. The closer . . . the warmer
3. The sharper . . . the easier
4. The noisier . . . the angrier
5. The faster . . . the more confused

◇ PRACTICE 21, p. 282.

1. (D) Kangaroos are the most familiar Australian grassland animals.
2. (C) Giraffes have the longest necks of all animals.
3. (F) Apes and monkeys are the most intelligent animals that live on land (besides human beings).
4. (E) Bottle-nosed dolphins are the most intelligent animals that live in water.
5. (B) African elephants have the largest ears of all animals.
6. (A) Horses have the largest eyes of all four-legged land animals.

◇ PRACTICE 22, p. 282.

1. the deepest ocean
2. the cleanest air
3. The highest mountains on earth
4. the biggest bird
5. The two greatest natural dangers
6. the most popular forms of entertainment
7. The three most common street names
8. The longest river in South America
9. the largest living animal

◇ PRACTICE 23, p. 283.

1. the laziest . . . in
2. the most nervous of
3. the most beautiful . . . in
4. the worst . . . in
5. the farthest/furthest . . . in
6. the best . . . of
7. the biggest . . . in
8. the oldest . . . in

9. the most comfortable . . . in
10. the most exhausted of

◇ PRACTICE 24, p. 283.

1. the best . . . have ever had
2. the most responsible . . . have ever known
3. the nicest . . . have ever had
4. the most difficult . . . have ever taken
5. the best . . . have ever tasted
6. the worst . . . have ever made
7. the most beautiful . . . have ever seen
8. the easiest . . . have ever taken

◇ PRACTICE 26, p. 285.

1. the worst
2. worse
3. the best
4. better
5. the worst
6. worse
7. the worst
8. better

◇ PRACTICE 29, p. 287.

1. heavier than . . . the heaviest . . . of
2. friendlier than
3. the most famous . . . in
4. more wheels than
5. easier . . . than
6. larger than . . . darker . . . than
7. the safest
8. faster . . . than
9. bigger than
10. the loudest . . . in
11. the largest . . . in . . . the smallest . . . of
12. more important than . . . less important than
13. more information
14. kinder . . . more generous
15. more honest . . . than
16. the worst
17. The most important
18. more education than
19. the longest
20. the most delightful
21. The harder . . . the more impossible
22. the most common/commonest . . . in
23. faster than . . . the fastest . . . of
24. larger than
25. The greatest . . . in
26. safer . . . than
27. the largest . . . in

◇ PRACTICE 31, p. 291.

1. to
2. as
3. from
4. Ø . . . Ø
5. to
6. as
7. from
8. Ø . . . Ø
9. to . . . Ø . . . as . . . from
10. Ø . . . as . . . Ø . . . to . . . from

◇ PRACTICE 32, p. 292.

1. different
2. similar
3. the same
4. alike . . . alike . . . different
5. like
6. different
7. like
8. A: similar   B: like . . . alike
9. A: as   B: the same
10. A: alike   B: similar . . . the same

Chapter 14   NOUN CLAUSES

◇ PRACTICE 1, p. 296.

1. I don't know <u>where Jack bought his new boots</u>.   NOUN CLAUSE
2. Where did Jack buy his new boots**?**   QUESTION
3. I don't understand <u>why Ann left</u>.   NOUN CLAUSE
4. Why did Ann leave**?**   QUESTION
5. I don't know <u>where your book is</u>.   NOUN CLAUSE
6. Where is your book**?**   QUESTION
7. When did Bob come**?**   QUESTION
8. I don't know <u>when Bob came</u>.   NOUN CLAUSE
9. What does "calm" mean**?**   QUESTION
10. Tarik knows <u>what "calm" means</u>.   NOUN CLAUSE
11. I don't know <u>how long the earth has existed</u>.   NOUN CLAUSE
12. How long has the earth existed**?**   QUESTION

◇ PRACTICE 2, p. 296.

Part I:

1. I don't know <u>where [Patty] [went] last night</u>.
2. Do you know <u>where [Joe's parents] [live]</u>?
3. I know <u>where [Joe] [lives]</u>.
4. Do you know <u>what time [the movie] [begins]</u>?
5. She explained <u>where [Brazil] [is]</u>.
6. I don't believe <u>what [Estefan] [said]</u>.
7. I don't know <u>when [the packages] [will arrive]</u>.
8. Please tell me <u>how far [it] [is] to the post office</u>.
9. I don't know <u>[who] [knocked] on the door</u>.
10. I wonder <u>[what] [happened] at the party last night</u>.

Part II:

1. Where did Patty go last night?
2. Where do Joe's parents live?
3. Where does Joe live?
4. What time does the movie begin?
5. Where is Pine Street?
6. What did Estefan say?
7. When will the packages arrive?
8. How far is it to the post office?
9. Who knocked on the door?
10. What happened at the party last night?

◇ PRACTICE 3, p. 298.

1. where Jim goes
2. where Alex went
3. why Maria is laughing
4. why fire is
5. how much a new Honda costs
6. why Mike is always
7. how long birds live
8. when the first wheel was invented
9. how many hours a light bulb burns
10. where Emily bought
11. who lives
12. who(m) Julie talked

◇ PRACTICE 4, p. 299.

1. A: Jason works . . . does he work
2. A: did Susan eat   B: she ate
3. A: does that camera cost   B: this camera costs
4. A: can you run   B: I can run
5. A: did you see   B: I saw
6. A: Mr. Gow's office is . . . is Mr. Gow's office
7. A: did she get   B: she got
8. A: is it   B: it is
9. A: will you know   B: I will know
10. A: do you go   B: Do you mean . . . you want . . . I go   A: other people go
11. A: Who invented   B: who invented
12. A: did Toshi borrow   B: Toshi borrowed
13. A: does Rachel plan/is Rachel planning   B: she will return   A: was she   B: she was
14. A: did Tom go   B: you said   A: Tom went

◇ PRACTICE 5, p. 301.

1. who [that man] [is]
2. [who] [called]
3. who [those people] [are]
4. who [that person] [is]
5. [who] [lives] next door to me
6. who [my teacher] [will be] next semester

$\overset{S}{}\overset{V}{}$

7. [who] [will teach] us next semester

$\overset{S}{}\overset{V}{}$

8. what [a lizard] [is]

$\overset{S}{}\overset{V}{}$

9. [what] [happened] in class yesterday

$\overset{S}{}\overset{V}{}$

10. whose hat [this] [is]

$\overset{S}{}\overset{V}{}$

11. [whose hat] [is] on the table

◇ PRACTICE 6, p. 301.

1. I don't know who that woman *is.*
2. I don't know who *is* on the phone.
3. I don't know what a crow *is.*
4. I don't know what *is* in that bag.
5. I don't know whose car *is* in the driveway.
6. I don't know whose car that *is.*
7. I don't know who Bob's doctor *is.*
8. I don't know who *is* in the doctor's office.

◇ PRACTICE 7, p. 301.

1. whose car that is
2. whose car is in front of Sam's house
3. who has the scissors
4. who the best students are
5. what a violin is
6. what causes earthquakes
7. what kind of fruit that is
8. whose hammer this is
9. who it is . . . where you are

◇ PRACTICE 10, p. 305.

1. if (whether) Tom is coming
2. if (whether) Jennifer can play the piano
3. if (whether) Paul went to work yesterday
4. if (whether) Susan is coming to work today
5. if (whether) Mr. Pips will be at the meeting
6. if (whether) Barcelona is a coastal town
7. if (whether) Carl would like to come with us
8. if (whether) I still have Yung Soo's address

◇ PRACTICE 15, p. 308.

1. I believe **that** we need to protect endangered species of animals.
2. Last night I dreamed **that** I was at my aunt's house.
3. I think **that** most people have kind hearts.
4. I know **that** Matt walks a long distance to school every day.
   I assume **that** he doesn't have a bicycle.
5. I heard **that** Sara dropped out of school.
6. Did you notice **that** Ji Ming wasn't in class yesterday? I hope **that** he's okay.
7. I believe **that** she told the truth.

8. A: Can Julia prove **that** her watch was stolen?
   B: I suppose **that** she can't, but she suspects **that** her roommate's friend took it.
9. A: Did you know **that** leopards sometimes keep their dead prey in trees?
   Yes, I understand **that** they save their food for later if they're not hungry.
10. A: Do you believe **that** a monster really exists in Loch Ness in Scotland?
    B: It says **that** some scientists have proved that the Loch Ness Monster exists.
    A: I think **that** the monster is purely fictional.

◇ PRACTICE 16, p. 309.

1. I'm sorry **that** you won't be here for Joe's party.
2. I'm glad **that** it's warm today.
3. I'm surprised **that** you bought a car.
4. Are you certain **that** Mr. McVay won't be here tomorrow?
5. John is pleased **that** Claudio will be here for the meeting.
6. Carmella was convinced **that** I was angry with her, but I wasn't.
7. Jason was angry **that** his father wouldn't let him use the family car.
8. Andy was fortunate **that** you could help him with his algebra.
   He was delighted **that** he got a good grade on the exam.
9. It's a fact **that** the Nile River flows north.
10. It's true **that** some dinosaurs could fly.
11. Are you aware **that** dinosaurs lived on earth for one hundred and twenty-five million (125,000,000) years?
12. Is it true **that** human beings have lived on earth for only four million (4,000,000) years?

◇ PRACTICE 20, p. 312.

1. I don't think that Alice has a car.
2. I think that Alex passed his French course.
3. I hope that Mr. Kozari is going to be at the meeting.
4. I think that cats can swim.
5. I don't think that gorillas have tails.
6. I suppose that Janet will be at Omar's wedding.

Chapter 15   QUOTED SPEECH AND REPORTED SPEECH

◇ PRACTICE 1, p. 314.

1. Alex said, "**D**o you smell smoke?"
2. He said, "**S**omething is burning."
3. He said, "**D**o you smell smoke? **S**omething is burning."
4. Rachel said, "**T**he game starts at seven."
5. She said, "**T**he game starts at seven. **W**e should leave here at six."
6. She said, "**T**he game starts at seven. **W**e should leave here at six. **C**an you be ready to leave then?"

◇ **PRACTICE 2, p. 315.**
1. "Do you smell smoke?" **A**lex said.
2. "Something is burning," he said.
3. "Do you smell smoke? **S**omething is burning," he said.
4. "The game starts at seven," Rachel said.
5. "The game stasrts at seven. **W**e should leave here at six," she said.
6. "Can you be ready to leave at six?" she asked.
7. "The game starts at seven. **W**e should leave here at six. **C**an you be ready to leave then?" she said.
8. "The game starts at seven," she said. "**W**e should leave here at six. **C**an you be ready to leave then?"

◇ **PRACTICE 3, p. 315.**
1. Mrs. Hill said, "**M**y children used to take the bus to school."
2. She said, "**W**e moved closer to the school."
3. "Now my children can walk to school," Mrs. Hill said.
4. "Do you live near the school?" she asked.
5. "Yes, we live two blocks away," I replied.
6. "How long have you lived here?" Mrs. Hill wanted to know.
7. I said, "**W**e've lived here for five years. **H**ow long have you lived here?"
8. "We've lived here for two years," Mrs. Hill said. "**H**ow do you like living here?"
9. "It's a nice community," I said. "**I**t's a good place to raise children."

◇ **PRACTICE 4, p. 316.**
CONVERSATION 1:
    "Why weren't you in class yesterday?" Mr. Garcia asked me.
    "I had to stay home and take care of my pet bird," I said. "He wasn't feeling well."
    "What? Did you miss class because of your pet bird?" Mr. Garcia demanded to know.
    I replied, "Yes, sir. That's correct. I couldn't leave him alone. He looked so miserable."
    "Now I've heard every excuse in the world!" Mr. Garcia said. Then he threw his arms in the air and walked away.

CONVERSATION 2:
    "Both of your parents are deaf, aren't they?" I asked Robert.
    "Yes, they are," he replied.
    "I'm looking for someone who knows sign language," I said. "Do you know sign language?" I asked.
    "Of course I do. I've been using sign language with my parents since I was a baby," he said. "It's a beautiful and expressive language. I often prefer it to spoken language."
    "Well, a deaf student is going to visit our class next Monday. Could you interpret for her?" I asked.
    "That's great!" he answered immediately and enthusiastically. "I'd be delighted to. I'm looking forward to meeting her. Can you tell me why she is coming?"
    "She's interested in seeing what we do in our English classes," I said.

◇ **PRACTICE 7, p. 318.**
1. he . . . his
2. I . . . my
3. she . . . her
4. he . . . me
5. she . . . my
6. they . . . their
7. he . . . his
8. he . . . me . . . him . . . his

◇ **PRACTICE 8, p. 318.**
1. needed
2. was meeting
3. had studied
4. had forgotten
5. was
6. would carry
7. could teach
8. had to attend
9. should leave
10. wanted

◇ **PRACTICE 10, p. 320.**
1. told
2. said
3. said
4. told
5. told
6. told
7. told
8. said
9. told
10. said

◇ **PRACTICE 11, p. 321.**
1. how old I was
2. if he was going to be
3. if I could hear
4. if he had ever seen
5. if she was passing her
6. if she had
7. when he would be back from his
8. if he had changed his

◇ **PRACTICE 15, p. 324.**
1. asked . . . to help
2. invited . . . to have
3. encouraged . . . to take
4. advised . . . to call . . . (to) apologize
5. permitted . . . to use
6. ordered . . . to sit
7. reminded . . . to order
8. warned . . . not to go

◇ **PRACTICE 20, p. 329.**
1. A
2. B
3. B
4. C
5. B
6. C
7. A
8. B
9. C
10. B
11. C
12. B

Chapter 16 USING WISH; USING IF

◇ PRACTICE 1, p. 333.
1. NO—She wishes she were safe at home.
2. YES—He wishes he had not come to the woods.
3. NO—Heidi wishes she could remember how to get back to town.
4. NO—Sara wishes she had listened to her mother.
5. NO—David wishes he had a flashlight.
6. YES—Heidi wishes they had not left the main path.

◇ PRACTICE 2, p. 334.
1. had
2. didn't have
3. taught
4. didn't snow
5. understood
6. could sing
7. didn't have . . . had
8. didn't have to study
9. were
10. were

◇ PRACTICE 3, p. 334.
1. don't . . . did
2. do . . . didn't
3. isn't . . . were
4. doesn't . . . did
5. am . . . weren't
6. can't . . . could

◇ PRACTICE 4, p. 335.
1. had had
2. hadn't had
3. had understood
4. hadn't lost
5. had been

◇ PRACTICE 5, p. 335.
1. did . . . hadn't
2. didn't . . . had
3. did . . . hadn't
4. don't . . . did
5. am . . . weren't

◇ PRACTICE 7, p. 336.
1. NO . . . NO—had . . . could build
2. NO . . . YES—were . . . would not be
3. NO . . . NO—had . . . could lead
4. NO . . . YES—had listened . . . would not have come
5. YES . . . YES-had not left . . . would not have gotten

◇ PRACTICE 8, p. 337.
1. were . . . could speak
2. didn't have . . . would ask
3. needed . . . would buy
4. wasn't . . . would finish
5. had . . . could go
6. were . . . could paint
7. understood . . . could solve

◇ PRACTICE 10, p. 338.
1. need . . . will/can buy
2. needed . . . would/could buy
3. had needed . . . would have/could have bought
4. go . . . will/can see
5. went . . . would/could see
6. had gone . . . would have/could have seen
7. have . . . will/can write
8. had . . . would/could write
9. had had . . . would have/could have written

◇ PRACTICE 11, p. 339.
1. had gone . . . would/could have finished
2. would have answered . . . had heard
3. had told . . . would/could have helped
4. would/could have seen . . . had come
5. had read . . . could have talked
6. had seen . . . would/could have offered
7. had not had to get . . . would/could have completed

◇ PRACTICE 12, p. 339.
1. you'd = you had
   I'd = I would
2. I'd = I would
3. I'd (known) = I had (known
   I'd (have bought) = I would (have bought)
4. he'd = he would
5. I'd = I had
   They'd = They would

◇ PRACTICE 13, p. 340.
1. D	6. C
2. B	7. B
3. C	8. A
4. D	9. D
5. A	10. D

◇ PRACTICE 15, p. 341.
1. hadn't been	6. hadn't yelled
2. wouldn't have found	7. wouldn't have been found
3. hadn't yelled	8. hadn't known
4. had walked	9. would have had to spend
5. wouldn't have heard	10. hadn't gone

◇ PRACTICE 17, p. 342.
1. had . . . would take
2. were . . . would/could build
3. were . . . would look
4. watch
5. is/will be . . . would be
6. would rise
7. were . . . would the rainbow be . . . would be
8. A: stay/will stay   B: would stay
9. would you do . . . were . . . Would you run . . . Would you call . . . Would you use
10. would you do . . . were
11. A: had   B: had . . . could carry . . . (could) pick
12. would take